WOMEN
AT THE CROSS

WOMEN
AT THE CROSS

EXPERIENCING *the* WONDER *and*
MYSTERY *of* CHRIST'S LOVE

LINDA
LESNIEWSKI

R Revell
Grand Rapids, Michigan

© 2005 by Linda Lesniewski

Published by Revell
a division of Baker Publishing Group
P.O. Box 6287, Grand Rapids, MI 49516-6287
www.revellbooks.com

Paperback edition published 2008

Previously published under the title *Drawn to the Cross*

Printed in the United States of America

Library of Congress Cataloging-in-Publication Data
Lesniewski, Linda, 1949–
    [Drawn to the cross]
    Women at the cross : experiencing the wonder and mystery of Christ's
love / Linda Lesniewski.
        p.   cm.
    Includes bibliographical references (p.   ).
    ISBN 978-0-8007-3243-1 (pbk.)
    1. Women in the Bible. 2. Jesus Christ—Friends and associates. 3. Bible.
N.T. Gospels—Criticism, interpretation, etc. I. Title.
BS2445.L47 2008
270.082—dc22   2007041264

Scripture is taken from the HOLY BIBLE, NEW INTERNATIONAL VERSION®. NIV®. Copyright © 1973, 1978, 1984 by International Bible Society. Used by permission of Zondervan. All rights reserved.

Contents

Contents

Acknowledgments

This book, like most, is a product of many collaborative efforts. I want to especially express my appreciation to my husband, Gary. His gifted teaching of God's Word has shown me how to approach it with both reverence and scholarship. His personal encouragement made it possible for me to step out in faith. Without his support, I would have neither begun nor completed the journey!

Special appreciation also goes to Anne Murchison. After I shared my initial observation of the women at the crucifixion, Anne immediately took action by whisking me off to my first writer's conference! She's remained my faithful mentor and cheerleader throughout the whole process.

The contributing authors of www.encouraging.com have been fellow pilgrims as we grow in our understanding of the writing process. Georgia Andrus, Carol Conser, Pat Eppler, Melissa Fisher, Stacy Graves, Mary Ann Lackland, Jo Parks, Nancy Paul, Nancy Shirah, Lynda Speak, Pam Thedford, and Janice Yandell provided encouragement through their own love of writing and their belief in the ministry of the written word.

The LifeWay Ministry Multipliers, under the leadership of Chris Adams, not only model a lifestyle of living at the foot of the cross but also model the same devotion to Jesus Christ as the women at the crucifixion. I consider you journey-mates in our spiritual pilgrimage. Your friendship bolsters my faith and courage.

My supportive colleagues, the staff of Green Acres Baptist Church, have mentored me in serving God through his work in the local church. In many ways they have welcomed my presence much like the disciples welcomed the presence of the women who followed and served Christ. I appreciate you guys!

To my editor, Vicki Crumpton, a heartfelt thank you for your vision and patience. Your biblical studies and professional expertise enhance your natural coaching abilities! I'm blessed by your friendship and the focus of your life.

A special thank you goes to Karen and Richard DeLeon for sharing their get-away cabin in New Mexico. That critical period of uninterrupted writing was not only productive but also revitalizing!

Special appreciation goes to Lynda Speak, who cheerfully invested tireless hours in proofing and re-proofing! What an amazing gift! Mary Ann Lackland offered professional guidance as I initially struggled to organize my thoughts. My sister, Claudia Walker, composed a pen and ink sketch portraying women through the ages who have faithfully followed and served Christ. Thanks, Claudia. It was just the visual I needed to finish developing my thoughts. In addition, I owe a special thank you to Nancy Paul, who composed inspirational verses for each chapter and to Pam Thedford, who provides ongoing prayer support.

I also want to express my appreciation to Lori, Nathan, Lisa, and Jonathan, who never complained about a mom distracted with the task at hand! Even though much of my writing occurred during the initial season of an empty nest, they still had to adjust to a mother who arrived for a visit with a laptop.

Finally, words are inadequate to express my devotion to Jesus Christ, the Living Word, who provides in Scripture everything we need for living. In my feeble attempt to explore the depths of God's gift of salvation, I've discovered new levels of his love for me, a woman—and I will be forever changed.

Introduction

After completing a two-year sojourn through *My Utmost for His Highest* by Oswald Chambers, I struggled with his challenge to "get back to the bedrock of the Cross of Christ." For in doing so, he said, "you set loose the energy of God!" He continued in his formal English to challenge his listeners "to consider bare-spirited the tragedy of God" as you "brood upon the tragedy of God upon the cross."[1]

I winced at the thought. I dread Easter messages detailing the agony and torture of Christ. My heart recoils and my mind just tunes out! I prefer the children's version—the same one I've told to first graders for fifteen years. Small objects hidden in numbered plastic eggs communicate the story from Jesus riding a donkey into Jerusalem to Jesus ascending to heaven. In telling the story, I can move quickly through the traumatic parts and on to the happy ending, the resurrection!

Oswald Chambers's challenge to bring myself "back to the bedrock of the Cross of Christ" seriously impacted me. For days I pondered how the cross could "set loose the energy of God" in my life and in the lives of other women. How could God draw women to Christ's crucifixion and the work he accomplished there?

Then I remembered that some women actually attended the crucifixion. They experienced firsthand the whole tragedy. They heard the buzz of the flies and breathed the dust of the passing crowds. They didn't just hear the crucifixion story while sitting on padded pews in an air-conditioned church.

So began my personal journey. I started reading the Gospel accounts from the perspective of the women standing at the scene of the crucifixion. During the process, I surprisingly discovered different listings of women in each of the Gospels. I eventually had to grab a pen and write down the names to help keep them straight. I discovered the names of four women, a fifth woman identified as the sister of Mary, Jesus's mother, and two women whose presence is inferred. In addition, all the Gospels included a reference to other women.

Throughout the next few weeks, I wondered why I had previously missed these women's presence at the crucifixion. I never included them in my Easter Egg Story presentation nor heard them discussed in Easter sermons. I had a lot of questions. Who were these women? Why did they come, and why did they stay? What held them there when others fled? What did they see? What did they feel? Why did God see that their presence was recorded in Scripture? What could I learn from them that would draw me and other women to the cross? And what had drawn women throughout the last two thousand years back to the scene of the crucifixion?

The following pages contain my findings and conclusions as well as topics for small group discussions. I was surprised by what I learned and by what I felt—spiritual kinship with the women who stood there that day as well as with those drawn to the cross through the years. By the time I finished my personal study, I felt like I too had worshiped with them at the cross.

In addition, I've experienced a new depth of love for Jesus and a rekindled gratitude for his obedience to death on the cross. Now I extend an invitation to you to join me in observing with our earliest sisters in Christ the wonders and mysteries of his love.

PART 1

THE CRUCIFIXION
OF CHRIST

Observe the crucifixion of Christ through the events of the six hours at Calvary. Meet the women who silently agonized nearby throughout the day. Examine their culture, personal struggles, and devotion to Christ. Consider how the emotions present at the crucifixion might mirror your own as you reflect on Christ's death. Finally, join with the women as they offer a gift of love and devotion to their dying Savior.

1

The Crucifixion Scene

Some women were watching from a distance.

Mark 15:40

Mary Magdalene, Joanna, Susanna, Mary the mother of James and Joses, Mary the mother of Jesus, Mary's sister, and Salome had arrived in Jerusalem with Jesus and the disciples from Galilee to celebrate the Passover feast. In Galilee they had traveled with Jesus to care for his needs. They also helped to support Jesus and the disciples out of their own financial resources. Together that day they witnessed a Roman execution, a crucifixion—a torturous death reserved for criminals and slaves.

The site was close to the city, just outside the northwest city wall where festival pilgrims and residents passed on public roads—providing a poignant deterrent to crime. Locals called the limestone mound the Place of the Skull, or in Aramaic, Golgotha.

Romans, seeking maximum exposure, posted permanent upright beams near the base of the hill at street level. The rugged rocky outcropping, later known as Calvary, served as a backdrop for the greatest drama of all time.

The women witnessed Roman soldiers methodically carry out their grizzly task of executing two thieves and the Son of God. They saw Jesus refuse wine mixed with myrrh, a painkiller readily accepted by the other two. Clothes, rudely stripped, exposed nakedness to the jeering crowd. Arms, nailed at the wrists and secured with rope, suspended the limp figure. Sweaty soldiers lifted and secured the rough-hewn crossbeams in a notch on the upright post. One rusty spike pierced both feet just above the ankle. A plaque stating Christ's crime hung above his head. In Aramaic, Greek, and Latin, it said, "JESUS OF NAZARETH, THE KING OF THE JEWS" (John 19:19).

Nine till noon, the women watched the Passover throngs file past the cross. Jesus, hanging just a few feet off the ground, provided an accessible target for their sneers, insults, and scorn. In passing they shouted, "He saved others; let him save himself if he is the Christ of God, the Chosen One" (Luke 23:35). "You, who are going to destroy the temple and build it in three days, come down from the cross and save yourself!" (Mark 15:29–30).

The chief priests and teachers of the law also mocked him among themselves, saying, "Let this Christ, this King of Israel, come down now from the cross, that we may see and believe"

(Mark 15:32). Even one of the crucified criminals scoffed, "Aren't you the Christ? Save yourself and us!" (Luke 23:39).

The women watched as soldiers carefully sorted Jesus's clothing and other meager possessions into four piles—compensation for each soldier's work. Jesus's tunic, woven out of one piece of cloth and not easily divided, prompted a quick game of chance. After gathering small stones from the ground, bantering soldiers tossed their dice—grown men playing games at the feet of God.

By noon, when most of the passersby had returned to their holiday preparations, this small band of faithful women experienced an unnatural encroaching darkness. The rays of the sun dimmed and blackness crept over the land. They huddled closer and held tightly to one another as this ominous miracle of nature transpired.

Later in the day, a small cluster of women broke away from the distant crowd. Moving cautiously, they eased past the soldiers to stand close to the cross. From there, Mary the mother of Jesus, Mary's sister,[1] Mary the wife of Clopas, and Mary Magdalene could see and hear Jesus clearly. The apostle John, having arrived at the scene, stood with them. Upon looking down and seeing his mother, Jesus said, "Dear woman, here is your son," and to John, "Here is your mother" (John 19:26–27). Silence followed, interrupted only by his labored intermittent breathing.

About three o'clock the women heard Jesus cry out through the darkness, *"Eloi, Eloi, lama sabachthani?"* which means "My God, my God, why have you forsaken me?" (Mark 15:34).[2] The pungent odor of vinegary wine lightly scented the air as a soldier lifted a soaked sponge to his lips. They heard Jesus call out, "Father, into your hands I commit my spirit" (Luke 23:45), followed by, "It is finished" (John 19:30). Then, as the heavens mourned in darkness, the earth cried out its own agony. It moaned and groaned with rumblings and loud quakes. Boulders crashed and tombs broke open. The centurion's own proclamation followed with a terrifying and desperate realization, "Surely he was the Son of God" (Matt. 27:54).

The remaining crowd left silently, beating their breasts, a common response to despair. But as the gathering continued to thin, the women remained, watching. Suddenly heads turned toward the clanking of metal armor as more soldiers arrived. One barked Pilate's order to break the criminals' legs. Doing so prevented using their legs to push upward to fill their lungs with air, hastening death by asphyxiation. The crack of bone against boards jolted the stillness, as did the whine of a sword drawn swiftly from its sheath. Since Jesus had already died, a Roman soldier pierced Jesus's side, confirming his death— one last insult that brought forth a "sudden flow of blood and water" (John 19:34).

Evening approached, and Sabbath preparations demanded completion before sundown arrived around six o'clock. Only two women remained to see Joseph and Nicodemus arrive unexpectedly to claim Jesus's body from the cross. They heard the rustle of linen and smelled the aroma of spices as the men hastily wrapped the corpse and carried it to a nearby tomb—as darkness came for the second time that day.

Who were these women arriving from Galilee with Jesus? What compelled them to witness his crucifixion and burial? What drew them to the foot of the cross? And, most of all, why did they remain when others fled?

2

The Women
and Their World

Many other women who had come up with him to
Jerusalem were also there.

Mark 15:41

We know several significant things about the women
who witnessed the crucifixion. We know names or
identities and the area of Palestine from which they traveled.
We have information on their culture, religion, and tradi-
tions, as well as records of previous encounters with Christ.
These earlier interactions with Jesus combined with profiles
of their world help us to better understand their deep level
of commitment and devotion.

Position in Judaism

From historical writings, we know that Judaism in Jesus's time held a low opinion of women. Joy reigned at the birth of a boy, but the birth of a daughter brought indifference or even sorrow. A woman's value in the Jewish community was based mostly on her ability to bear children. A commonly repeated formula, "Women, slaves, and children,"[1] clearly communicated their position in society. Another example of the status of women comes from a prayer recommended for daily use. The prayer of thanksgiving simply says, "Blessed [be God] that hath not made me a woman."[2] Another example of status comes from this guideline: "In a case of danger to life, the husband must be saved first unless the wife's chastity is threatened."[3]

During worship at the synagogue services, women participated in a separate section located behind a lattice barrier. Later the religious rulers increased the separation by building a gallery with a special entrance for women. Furthermore, women did not join in the liturgical service—they simply listened. In the Jerusalem temple, women could go no farther than into the Court of the Gentiles and Court of Women. Levitical law even kept women from these designated areas during their monthly menstruation. This limitation also included a period of forty days after the birth of a son and eighty days after the birth of a daughter (Lev. 12:2–5; Luke 2:22).

Opportunity for religious instruction was limited to boys and men. Writings from AD 90 inform us, "If a man gives his daughter knowledge of the Law, it is as though he taught her lechery," and "Better to burn the Torah than to teach it to a woman."[4] Even though only boys attended schools, girls in the higher social class families occasionally received a secular education, usually learning Greek.[5]

Marriage

Old Testament law also gave direction for Jewish marriages. Parents chose a mate for their son, perhaps consulting with him to see if he approved of their choice. The father of the young man then spoke with the father of the chosen bride, and together they determined a price to be paid or services to be given to the father of the bride as compensation for the loss of a worker.

Jews commonly married at a young age, which made the parents' choice of a mate simply a practical matter. By New Testament times, the Jewish leaders had decided to establish minimum ages for marriage contracts, setting the ages at thirteen for boys and twelve for girls—children by today's standards. Romance before marriage did occasionally exist, but it played a minor role in the lives of teenagers. Jews believed love began at marriage. You did not marry the person you loved; you loved the mate you married.

The length of engagement varied. Sometimes the couple married the same day of engagement. Often, however, a period of time elapsed between betrothal and the marriage ceremony. During this time, the young man prepared a place in his father's house for his bride, which usually meant adding on a bedroom. Before marriage a young woman remained shut away from the outer world, submissive to the power of her father. After marriage she remained mostly isolated and submissive to a new authority, her husband.

Domestic Life

Domestic chores required strength and energy. Women devoted many hours each day to meal preparation, especially grinding grain for baking. They often worked additional hours in the evening to prepare flour for the next day's baking. Unless they had daughters, they had no assistance with the grinding, because men considered it an insulting or humiliating task.

Not only did women grind the grain, churn the butter, and prepare the meals, they also drew all the household water, carrying heavy pitchers back to their homes on their heads. Along with water, a farmer's wife would also transport heavy loads of fuel, flat cakes of dried dung and straw, back to her home on her head.

Women also spun wool, wove cloth, and sewed the family clothes. Occasionally they sold surplus woven or hand-stitched items to assist with the family's income, but their husbands had rights to all of their earnings. On top of manual labor, a wife also had responsibilities often relegated to servants, washing her husband's face, hands, and feet.

Despite the challenges of married life, married women lived with the fear of widowhood. Without a husband as protector and provider, a widow commonly fell prey to unscrupulous men and had to depend on the law for protection. Widows without children traditionally returned to their parents' home because they had no way to protect or provide for themselves.

The Women of Jerusalem

Historians must look diligently to locate female names in the Judeo-Roman world. Once found, they're quite limited in diversity. In fact, only three names account for 46 percent of all known names of that period, Maria, Salome, and Shelamzion.[6]

The scarcity of written women's names makes the listing of the women at Jesus's crucifixion all the more unusual. The Gospel writers supply the names of four women, three with the common name of Mary: Mary the mother of Jesus, Mary Magdalene, Salome, and Mary the wife of Clopas. In addition, we can assume Joanna's and Susanna's presence from supporting scriptural passages.[7] John the apostle provided the identity of a seventh woman, the sister of the mother of Jesus.

The Gospels of Matthew, Mark, and Luke include references to "many other women" present at the crucifixion (Matt. 27:55–56; Mark 15:40–41; Luke 23:49). These other women consisted of two distinct groups—residents of Jerusalem and Passover pilgrims.

Some of the women who lived in Jerusalem followed Jesus as he carried his crossbeam through the crowded streets. A portion of this group represented socially conscious volunteers who provided strong wine mixed with myrrh, which deadened pain and consciousness—the same mixture Jesus declined on the cross (Mark 15:23). Others came because they knew Jesus and had listened as he taught in the city of Jerusalem.

Jesus stopped when he heard these women's cries, despite his own weakness and pain. Turning and speaking directly to them, he moved the focus from his desperate situation to their own. Prophesying, he said, "Daughters of Jerusalem, do not weep for me; weep for yourselves and for your children. For the time will come when you will say, 'Blessed are the barren women, the wombs that never bore and the breasts that never nursed'" (Luke 23:28–29).

These women wept for Jesus but would have more reason to weep for themselves when the Romans fulfilled this prophecy in AD 70. Roman soldiers would kill more than 600,000 residents of Jerusalem—leaving only the towers of Herod's palace and part of the temple's western wall standing among the smoldering ruins.[8]

Passover Pilgrims

The rest of the women at the crucifixion either came with Jesus to Jerusalem from Galilee or traveled from other areas to attend the Passover celebration as required by Jewish law—exempting only pregnant women, nursing women, or women with small children from the pilgrimage.[9]

The Passover pilgrims included those women who accompanied Jesus to Jerusalem.[10] In serving and supporting him, they would have assisted with routine daily needs like trips to the market and meal preparation. Yet their presence with Christ and the apostles also allowed them a unique privilege—to receive the same teaching and training traditionally reserved for men.

The women witnessed Christ's miracles, healings, and intense discussions with religious rulers. As a result, they experienced many of the events recorded in Scripture and some of the "other things" John referred to when he wrote, "Jesus did many other things as well. If every one of them were written down, I suppose that even the whole world would not have room for the books that would be written" (John 21:25).

Combining historical information with Jewish culture and tradition allows us to piece together profiles of the women attending the crucifixion. In turn, these profiles help us see them as real women with real needs. Still, there is more to discover about each woman to help us understand the source of their passionate devotion to Christ.

3

The Women from Galilee

> Some women were watching from a distance.
> Among them were Mary Magdalene, Mary the
> mother of James the younger and of Joses, and
> Salome. In Galilee these women had followed him
> and cared for his needs.
>
> Mark 15:40–41

In addition to the residents of Jerusalem and the Passover
pilgrims at the crucifixion, we also find seven women identified as those who "followed him and cared for his needs"
(Mark 15:41).

Mary the Mother of Jesus

The most well known woman at the crucifixion was Mary the mother of Jesus. Mary lived as a peasant girl in Nazareth—until the angel Gabriel's announcement, "You will be with child and give birth to a son. . . . He will be great and will be called the Son of the Most High" (Luke 1:31–32). Even though the conception and birth of the long-awaited Messiah changed her life forever, she still lived and raised Jesus in relative obscurity until he left for public ministry.

Many believe Joseph, Mary's husband, died while Jesus was still young. Scripture last mentions Joseph during their family's trip to Jerusalem when Jesus, age twelve, remained behind in Jerusalem when the family left for Nazareth. After returning to Jerusalem and searching three days, Mary's frustration erupted. Her words indicated a mother's natural anxiety as well as a lack of understanding of Jesus's mission. "Son, why have you treated us like this? Your father and I have been anxiously searching for you" (Luke 2:48).

Jesus's response implied that "Mary should have gained a sense of his special filial relationship to God the Father."[1] In reply, he asked, "Why were you searching for me? Didn't you know I had to be in my Father's house?" (Luke 2:49). Luke adds, "But [Joseph and Mary] did not understand what he was saying to them" (Luke 2:50).

Once again, at the wedding in Cana, Mary demonstrated a lack of understanding of Jesus's unique mission when she reported to him, "They have no more wine" (John 2:3). Authors Tucker and Liefeld conclude, "Mary had to learn to follow him as a disciple rather than possessing and directing him as his mother."[2]

Later, when Jesus taught in a home in Capernaum, Mary and Jesus's brothers arrived and sent someone in to call for him. Jesus responded with words clarifying their new relationship. His mothers and brothers were now "whoever does God's will" (Mark 3:35).

By the end of Christ's three-year ministry, Mary would have been in her mid to late forties. She often traveled with Jesus, even though her other sons did not. She came with him, the disciples, and the other women to Jerusalem for the annual Passover feast.

Mary would have heard of Christ's arrest from the disciples later that same evening. Arriving the next morning, she followed the jeering mob and wailing women to the crucifixion site. Mary stood in the distance supported by the other women throughout the long excruciating day.

Mary Magdalene

Mary Magdalene lived in Magdala, a town on the western shore of the Sea of Galilee.[3] According to the culture, the order of names in a list indicated status or importance. Thus, Mary Magdalene must have possessed leadership abilities, because all four of the Gospel writers name her first when grouped with others.[4] Mary Magdalene clearly displayed strong leadership among the women as Peter did among the apostles.

Luke records that Christ freed Mary from seven demons (Luke 8:2). Although we don't know what characteristics of demon possession Mary manifested, we do have a few insights. Boyd Luter and Kathy McReynolds write in their book *Women as Christ's Disciples*, "It was quite obvious to those around her that

31

something was desperately wrong. The most vivid description of multiple demon possession in the Gospels is of a man from the region of the Gerasenes who met Jesus on the shores of the Sea of Galilee. . . . Night and day among the tombs and in the hills he would cry out and cut himself with stones (Mark 5:5)." This is a picture of a man who was in unspeakable agony and a community who greatly feared him. It could be that Mary Magdalene experienced some of these same horrors. Perhaps she too wailed and cut herself as she wandered aimlessly down Magdala's streets and alleys, her torn and dirty clothing matching the misery of her life. However it was, there is little doubt that her release from bondage was dramatic and life-changing. Her gratitude was manifested immediately by her devotion as a follower of Christ and her willingness to support him from her personal resources.[5]

This same Mary played a visible role in the crucifixion drama. She joined the small gathering of women that moved closer to the cross where she witnessed some of Christ's last words. She also lingered at the tomb after Christ's burial and revisited the grave early Sunday morning. There the resurrected Christ chose to reveal himself to Mary Magdalene and her friends. Christ also sent her from the tomb with a personal commission: "Go and tell my brothers to go to Galilee; there they will see me" (Matt. 28:10).

Salome

Salome's husband, Zebedee, owned a fishing business on the northeast shore of the Sea of Galilee.[6] There is little doubt their home had lively and loud days as their two sons, whom

Jesus later named "the sons of thunder," grew to manhood. Scriptural clues suggest that Salome possessed both social status and financial resources. Mark 1:20 mentions that Zebedee, her husband, had hired men working for him—a possible indicator of a thriving business. In addition, one son, John, received permission to enter the home of Annas, the high priest, during Jesus's questioning. Any family known by the high priest commanded respect and social status among the religious community. Last, Salome supported Jesus and his disciples out of her resources—even though Jewish women had little direct access to family finances.

Many people remember Salome as the mother who requested special favors for her two sons. "Grant that one of these two sons of mine may sit at your right and the other at your left in your kingdom" (Matt. 20:21). But others remember Salome for her sons' devotion to Christ. We certainly see the influence of a godly mother on their lives.

John, known as the beloved disciple, closely identified with the heart and teaching of Christ. John witnessed Jesus's transfiguration and accompanied Jesus farther into the Garden of Gethsemane (Matt. 17:1–2; 26:36–37). Jesus even entrusted his mother's care to John. Because of this, if Salome and Mary lived long lives, they might have shared John's personal care during their later years. In addition, just as Salome had supported Mary in the death of her son, so Mary likely had the opportunity to comfort Salome when James died as the first martyred apostle slain by a sword at Herod Agrippa's command in AD 44 (Acts 12:2).

Next to Christ's mother, Salome stands as the most notable mother involved in Jesus's ministry. Salome must have loved the Lord passionately to leave the comforts of her home and serve with her finances, her sons, and her life—and with her presence even as he died.

Joanna

Joanna enjoyed special privileges as the wife of Herod Antipas's personal household steward. Her husband held a high position of responsibility, serving the Roman ruler responsible for beheading John the Baptist. The night of Christ's arrest, this same Herod ridiculed Jesus by dressing him in a kingly robe before returning him to Pilate (Matt. 27:27–31; Luke 23:11).

Joanna lived with her husband, Cuza, in Tiberias on the Sea of Galilee. From there Herod ruled the regions of Galilee and Perea in Palestine.[7] During special feast days, Herod and his staff relocated to his Jerusalem palace. Her husband's job gave Joanna an excellent opportunity for witnessing in the palace among the servants.

Luke lists Joanna as one of three women followers Jesus healed. And he mentions her as a financial supporter of Jesus and his disciples. "Jesus traveled about from one town and village to another, proclaiming the good news of the kingdom of God. The Twelve were with him, and also some women who had been cured of evil spirits and diseases: Mary (called Magdalene) from whom seven demons had come out; Joanna the wife of Cuza, the manager of Herod's household; Susanna; and many others. These women were helping to support them out of their own means" (Luke 8:1–3). From that time forward, Scripture notes Joanna's faithfulness to Christ. Just like Salome and Mary Magdalene, she gave unselfishly of her time, energy, and money to travel with Jesus and support his ministry.

Joanna lingered at the cross, witnessed the empty tomb, and proclaimed the Lord's resurrection. She stands in history as a woman with social position whose devotion to her Lord expressed itself in humble service.

Susanna

We have little information about Susanna, except that she knew Jesus's healing touch. She also traveled with and supported Jesus out of her own finances (Luke 8:1–3). We do, however, have three clues to create a brief silhouette of her life. She had wealth and freedom to travel. She had also known the despair of physical or mental illness. Since her husband is not mentioned, we can also assume she knew the hardships of life as a widow. We also know her heart, and that communicates the most important quality of all.

Mary the Wife of Clopas

Next we gather information on one of the three Marys identified at the crucifixion site, Mary "the mother of James the younger and of Joses" (Mark 15:40). The phrase "Mary the wife of Clopas" (John 19:25) also provides identifying information. Because the Greek name Clopas also translates "Alphaeus," some think she could also be the mother of the apostle "James the son of Alphaeus."[8]

Mary joined the women who moved closer to the cross and witnessed Jesus's dying directives to his mother and John. She also walked with the small funeral procession and saw where Jesus's body was laid. Then, early Sunday morning, Mary returned to the tomb with the other women. There she saw the resurrected Christ and worshiped at his feet.

Mary's Sister

John's Gospel records the names of the women who moved closer to the foot of the cross. "Near the cross of Jesus stood his mother, his mother's sister, Mary the wife of Clopas, and Mary Magdalene" (19:25).[9] Mary's sister had been a part of Jesus's life from the earliest days of Gabriel's announcement. She watched Jesus through the years playing with her children, his cousins. She saw Mary struggle with the hardships of widowhood and the wonder of mothering the Messiah.

Because we have no record of Mary the mother of Jesus attending the burial, we can assume both sisters left after Christ's death. This sister shared in the drama for more than thirty years, and she shared in it now—caring for Mary as only a sister could. She joined an amazing group of women gathered at the cross to witness the world's greatest drama unfold. Though these women represented diverse social classes, ethnic regions, and life experiences, they stood united in their deep devotion to their Lord—just as women would in the early years of the church and throughout the centuries that followed.

4

Passions at the Cross of Christ

> I tell you the truth, you will weep and mourn while the world rejoices. You will grieve, but your grief will turn to joy.
>
> John 16:20

In observing the crucifixion, we witness the inter-woven passions of grieving women and exultant religious rulers. The women simultaneously embraced their grief and resisted their exhaustion. In addition, they withstood displays of terrifying passions from those around them. Scripture offers the modern-day witness clues to assist in sorting through the emotional fervor. In understanding the women's emotions, we better understand our own when we too attend the crucifixion of Christ.

Bewilderment

Just days earlier, the women heard the loud voices of the crowd of disciples joyfully praising God for miracles they had witnessed, "Blessed is the king who comes in the name of the Lord! Peace in heaven and glory in the highest!" (Luke 19:38). They heard the Pharisees in the same joyous crowd tell Jesus to rebuke the disciples—and Jesus's reply, "I tell you, if they keep quiet, the stones will cry out" (Luke 19:40). They felt the press of the great Passover crowd coming from Jerusalem to welcome Jesus as their conquering king, the Promised One. Even the Pharisees acknowledged to one another, "Look how the whole world has gone after him!" (John 12:19).

Yesterday—applause. Today—death as a common criminal. Salome's request for her sons to sit at the right and left hand of Jesus, the ruling king, contradicted the bewildering reality of Jesus, the suffering servant on the cross.

Piercing Anguish, a Mother's Pain

Prophecy provides sobering insight into the personal pain of Mary the mother of Jesus. Many years earlier, she and her husband, Joseph, presented the infant Jesus at the temple. There they encountered Simeon, a righteous and devout Jew. Upon seeing the child, Simeon praised God and prophesied to Mary, saying, "A sword will pierce your own soul" (Luke 2:35).

The prophecy, though frightening, failed to describe the agony Mary felt as she watched her son die. "If we could get into this mother's heart and picture this scene at Calvary, it would make his sacrifice more real to us."[1] The piercing pain defied words. It halted her breathing, churned her stomach, and crumpled her legs. Mary certainly would have chosen her own death over her son's. In time Salome also would experience a mother's grief with the martyrdom of her son. Other mothers in the centuries to come would experience similar pain.

Anguish Preceding Joy

During the last Passover meal, Jesus used the analogy of childbirth to describe how his followers would experience his death—intense waves of pain and anguish followed by deep joy. He said, "A woman giving birth to a child has pain because her time has come; but when her baby is born she forgets the anguish because of her joy that a child is born into the world. So with you: Now is your time of grief, but I will see you again and you will rejoice, and no one will take away your joy" (John 16:21–22).

Even though elation would eventually replace their grief, the women's current anguish demanded full attention and drained their last ounce of strength. Just as contractions in childbirth grow in strength, each new development—from Christ's arrest to the final moments on the cross—intensified their emotional pain. Yet, unknowingly, their pain also drew them nearer to the fulfillment of their joy—worshiping a living Christ! Today we too struggle through the anguish of Christ's suffering and rejoice each time we revisit the empty tomb.

Numbing Grief

Besides wounded hearts and anguish, the women experienced the extreme grief Jesus had spoken of to the disciples:

"You will weep and mourn while the world rejoices" (John 16:20). They grieved as a mother mourning over the death of a child, as a devoted disciple over the death of a beloved teacher, as a friend over the loss of a companion, and as a Jew over the cruelty and injustice of Roman rule. But even more, they grieved as women who felt they had lost the acceptance and unconditional love Jesus offered them.

Within this relationship, each woman experienced something profound, something no one had experienced since sin entered the world—emotional intimacy with God. This intimacy embraced healing, acceptance, unconditional love, affirmation, and a life rich with purpose, and they grieved its loss.

Invasive Anger

Mary Magdalene and the rest of the women could not block out the shouts and insults of the religious leaders and guards. Mark records in his Gospel, "The chief priests and the teachers of the law mocked him among themselves. 'He saved others,' they said, 'but he can't save himself! Let this Christ, this King of Israel, come down now from the cross, that we may see and believe'" (15:31–32). Luke records that the rulers "sneered at him. . . . The soldiers also came up and mocked him." Even "one of the criminals who hung there hurled insults at him" (Luke 23:35–39).

Jesus had upset the religious leaders' false security of a religion based on following the law. He had called the Pharisees "blind fools" (Matt. 23:17), "whitewashed tombs . . . full of dead men's bones" (v. 27), "snakes" and "brood of vipers" (v. 33). Christ had created chaos in their temple when he had

40

driven out the money changers (Matt. 21:12). He had deliberately broken their Sabbath laws. Now the religious leaders reveled in the bitter pleasure of revenge. This same emotion would continue to escalate until it eventually snuffed out the life of each disciple—and it continues today.

Terror of Death

Executions assaulted all of the human senses. Bloodied knives and hammers, implements of Roman cruelty, bred terror where they lay. Even though darkness eventually offered relief to the women's eyes, it failed to provide reprieve from the sounds and smells of death. Vile cursing assailed their ears. Even in the shadows, the moans and groans of the crucified assailed them. The women tried to block their senses but could not, and neither can we as we observe Christ's suffering.

Then, when it seemed as if the women could bear no more, the very ground that supported them heaved. Matthew records, "When the centurion and those with him who were guarding Jesus saw the earthquake and all that had happened, they were terrified" (27:54). Crashing boulders from the hillside and the crowd's frantic screams united to produce terror in the women's hearts—as well as in the soldiers. In response, the women clung more tightly to one another for physical and emotional steadiness.

Abandonment

Christ hung dying. The women, deserted by the very one who filled the empty places in their hearts, felt abandoned, deserted, forsaken—numb. They had listened and learned at his feet. They had walked and talked together, mile after mile, day after day. They shared meals, laughter, and tears.

Everything familiar had vanished, including the disciples' voices. Even their future seemed empty, and their hearts weighed heavy with feelings of desertion and rejection. Where do you go and what do you do when the one you know and love leaves you through death?

Total Exhaustion

The previous night, the women had heard of Christ's arrest in the Garden of Gethsemane. Throughout the long night hours that followed, they tossed restlessly and prayerfully. As soon as the morning rays dispelled the darkness, they left hurriedly to find Jesus. They soon discovered the raucous crowd near Pilate's house and followed it beyond the city walls.

Matthew records that as the day passed, the soldiers rested: "And sitting down, they kept watch over him there" (27:36). But the women, despite their own hunger and thirst, stood for six long hours. Courageous, exhausted, and undeniably faithful, these women continued to serve their Lord, even as he died.

Expressions of Love

The women heard the familiarity of Christ's loving words when he prayed, "Father forgive them, for they do not know what they are doing" (Luke 23:34). In addition, during Christ's last moments, he provided for his mother's care. "When Jesus saw his mother there, and the disciple whom he loved standing nearby, he said to his mother, 'Dear woman, here is your son,' and to the disciple, 'Here is your mother'" (John 19:26–27). They also heard Jesus offer pardon to one thief when he said, "Today you will be with me in paradise" (Luke 23:43).

The expressions of love the women witnessed only added to the confusion they felt. Why would the Son of God do nothing to stop the greatest crime of all time? They would have more "why" questions in their spiritual journey—just as would all followers after them.

Our Own Emotions

The women felt confusion, anguish, terror, and abandonment—all shrouded in love for Christ. When we as women witness the scene of Christ's death, we too sometimes feel confusing emotions. How do you respond to the aversion you experience when viewing Jesus's bloodied thorn-pierced brow and nail-pierced limbs?

Helplessness, guilt, anger, misplaced pity, and couldn't-there-be-some-other-way emotions can detour and distract our hearts. They can keep us from remembering that God will bring us through to a fresh, new, awe-inspiring understanding of his great love. So, stand as the women at the cross did among the pain and confusion. Remain faithful and steadfast.

5

The Women's Offering

All those who knew him, including the women who
had followed him from Galilee, stood at a distance,
watching these things.

Luke 23:49

Throughout the preceding years, the women had served
Jesus, and they served him now even as he died—and God
noticed. What did they bring to Calvary as their sacrificial
gift? Themselves. They stood, they waited, they saw. They
were simply "present."

The Gift of Emotional Presence

Luke records, "When all the people who had gathered to
witness this sight saw what took place, they beat their breasts

and *went away*. But all those who knew him, including the women who had followed him from Galilee, stood at a distance, watching these things" (Luke 23:48–49, emphasis added).[1] "Mark stresses that these women were afraid and troubled by what they witnessed, which makes it even more remarkable that they remained on the scene as long as they did."[2] Even in fear and grief, they served Jesus by their presence.

Luter and McReynolds point out that Mark's Gospel pays more attention to the female disciples than the males, which is "a truly remarkable proportion for a heavily patriarchal period of history."[3] I believe the Holy Spirit of God chose to record their attendance because their presence was important to Jesus. Observing Jesus's emotions preceding his death helps us to better understand the significance of the women's presence.

The Incarnation—Fully God, Fully Human

One of the great mysteries of the incarnation is that Christ was both fully divine and fully human. Jesus, in his humanity, experienced physical birth from a woman, growth, hunger, thirst, fatigue, sadness, and temptation just like us, yet he was without sin (Gal. 4:4; Luke 2:52; Matt. 4:2; John 19:28; 4:6; 11:35; Heb. 4:15). Yet Jesus was also fully God.

We see Christ's deity in his names—God, Son of God, Lord, King of Kings, and Lord of Lords (Heb. 1:8; Matt. 16:16; 26:61–64; 22:43–45; Rev. 19:16). His characteristics of omnipotence, omniscience, omnipresence, and immutability all attest to his divinity (Matt. 18:18, 20; John 1:48; Heb. 13:8). In addition, Christ's works on earth displayed the work of God. He created, sustained, forgave sin, raised the dead, judged, and sent the Holy Spirit (John 1:3; Col. 1:17; Luke 7:48; John 5:25, 27; 15:26). In "emptying himself," he became man.[4]

At the crucifixion, we observe both. Jesus suffered physically and emotionally as a human. He also suffered as God in experiencing judgment for sin so that we would not have to.

"You Will Leave Me All Alone"

The events that led up to the arrest and crucifixion provide a window into the fully human heart of Jesus and the expression of the need for human companionship. During the last Passover meal, Jesus said to his disciples, "A time is coming, and has come, when you will be scattered, each to his own home. You will leave me *all alone*" (John 16:32, emphasis added). A perceptive ear can hear the underlying sadness as Jesus anticipated abandonment by his disciples during a time of emotional need.

Matthew includes in his Gospel the prophecy from Zechariah that Christ quoted during his last evening with the disciples. "Strike the shepherd, and the sheep will be scattered" (Zech. 13:7). Christ knew he would accomplish the pinnacle of his work on earth without all of those he'd taught and loved at his side.

"Keep Watch with Me"

We quickly catch another glimpse of Jesus's humanity and emotional needs in the Garden of Gethsemane when he began to feel sorrowful and troubled. Jesus openly asked for the disciples' support. He wanted and needed their prayer. As his emotions threatened to overwhelm him, he sought the presence and encouragement of those closest to him. Taking Peter, James, and John aside, he said to them, "My soul is overwhelmed with sorrow to the point of death. Stay here and keep watch with me" (Matt. 26:38). Going a little farther, he fell to the ground and prayed as he struggled with deep sorrow and a troubled heart.

Christ's words "My soul is overwhelmed with sorrow to the point of death" suggest a sorrow so deep it almost kills. Revealing his deepest emotions gave his disciples compelling reasons to do what he asked—"Keep watch with me"—while he went a little farther to pray alone.

We hear disappointment in Christ's voice when he returned to find them asleep, "Could you men not keep watch with me for one hour?" (Matt. 26:40). Jesus asked his closest disciples to be physically present with him in his sorrow. He also asked them to pray so they would not fall into temptation—not only the distraction of sleep but also the spiritual defection Jesus predicted only hours earlier. Mark records that later, after Jesus's arrest, "everyone deserted him and fled" (14:50).

"Why Have You Forsaken Me?"

We hear the anguish in Christ's voice as he experienced for the first time in eternity the abandonment of his Father. Through the darkness of a mourning world, Jesus cried out, "My God, my God, why have you forsaken me?" (Mark 15:34). The mystery of what Jesus meant in this moment remains beyond our grasp. Jesus felt the horror of sin so deeply that for a time it obscured the intimate communion with his Father. Jesus's cry depicts his agony in experiencing for us the very essence of hell—separation from God.

Elizabeth Barrett Browning, in her poem "Cowper's Grave," expressed her own interpretation of Jesus's cry. "Immanuel's orphan'd cry his universe hath shaken. It went up single, echoless, 'My God, I am forsaken!'"

Why They Remained

During Christ's hours of abandonment, the women remained. Reflecting on who they were and their relationship with Christ helps us understand why they chose to stay despite their personal anguish and fear.

Jesus had touched each of these women's lives in a profound way. He filled a need for connectedness deep within their hearts. In a culture where women experienced social restrictions and isolation, he offered an intimate relationship with their Creator. Through Christ they'd personally known forgiveness, acceptance, affirmation, purpose, and hope—something unavailable to women since Eve's fall in the Garden of Eden. In response, they offered all they had to give—themselves.

In addition, the women responded as God had designed them to respond. Recent research reveals that during stress, men and women both experience an initial rush of adrenalin. While men respond with a fight or flight, women experience a secondary chemical response of oxytocin. This hormone influences women to nurture and gather with one another. God designed within women a caring, or "tending and befriending," response as a way to cope with stress,[5] and we see it in action at the cross.

We see it also during Christ's brief burial, at his tomb, and all throughout the work of the early church and beyond. We see that same "tending and befriending" response today as women demonstrate God's love to others during crises and as they continue to worship their Lord at the cross.

PART 2

EXPERIENCING THE RESURRECTION

J oin the band of followers as they form a small funeral procession for the Savior of the world. Travel back to the burial site with the women in the early morning hours, and rejoice with them as they discover the risen Christ. Celebrate the Good News and marvel at what God accomplished for humankind through the death and resurrection of his Son.

6

The Burial

Joseph took the body, wrapped it in a clean linen
cloth, and placed it in his own new tomb that he
had cut out of the rock.

Matthew 27:59–60

Jews rested on the Sabbath according to the commandment
God gave Moses—six days were for work, and the seventh
was for rest. Levitical law provided strict guidelines for defining
"rest." It described such things as the distance you could walk as
well as permissible and nonpermissible tasks. For instance, gathering wood or building a fire for cooking was not permitted.[1]

Even though Jews honored all Sabbaths, this approaching
Sabbath earned additional honor, for it coincided with the
first day of the Feast of Unleavened Bread. Out of respect

for the feast, the Jews wanted the soldiers to remove the dead bodies from the crosses before nightfall—the beginning of the Sabbath. Pilate agreed to hasten their death.

In response to Pilate's orders, soldiers grabbed metal rods and violently broke the criminals' legs on the left and right of Jesus. The broken legs prevented them from pushing up to fill their lungs—causing death by asphyxiation. When the soldiers came to Jesus, they discovered that he had already died. Instead of breaking his legs, one of the soldiers used his iron-tipped lance to pierce Jesus's side—an act of "good measure."[2]

Joseph of Arimathea

Joseph, a wealthy Jew from Arimathea, went boldly to Pilate to request Jesus's body. The bodies of all criminals, including Jesus's body, belonged to the Roman government. This made Joseph's request exceptionally bold and out of the ordinary. Joseph served on the prestigious council of the Sanhedrin in Jerusalem, the highest ruling body and court of justice among the Jews. As a secret follower of Christ, Joseph risked expulsion from the synagogue if exposed. Scripture also records that Joseph had not consented to the Sanhedrin's decision to seek Christ's death. Pilate, surprised to hear of Jesus's early death (Mark 15:44), summoned the centurion to confirm it—the same centurion who only moments earlier acknowledged, "Surely this was a righteous man" (Luke 23:47).

Because of Joseph's wealth and influential position on the Sanhedrin, Pilate granted permission for Jesus's burial instead of the routine disposal of corpses—the garbage heap or mass graves. Joseph hastily purchased linen cloth for the burial shroud and hurried to the crucifixion site outside the city walls. Nicodemus, another secret follower of Christ, assisted Joseph in removing the body from the cross and taking it to a nearby garden for burial preparations. The women from Galilee followed close behind them and watched.

Christ's Funeral Processional

The funeral procession for the King of the universe consisted of a few faithful followers, including Joseph of Arimathea, Nicodemus, Mary Magdalene, and Mary the wife of Clopas. The small procession quietly walked from Golgotha to Joseph's personal tomb close by.

Jewish burial customs included the washing, anointing, and shrouding of the body. Nicodemus and Joseph had only a short time before the Sabbath began and all labor ceased. Working quickly yet reverently, they closed Christ's eyes and straightened his arms by his sides. They brought water from the garden cistern and tenderly washed away the blood, the sweat, and the tears of their Savior.

They prepared the body by rubbing it with Nicodemus's lavish gift of powdered myrrh and aloes. Next they placed a linen cloth over his head, securing the chin. Then, beginning with his fingers, they tightly wrapped the linen strips around Christ's body, sprinkling aloe and myrrh between each strip.[3]

Joseph and Nicodemus strained as they stooped to carry the body through the low entrance of Joseph's tomb—a tomb "in which no one had ever been laid" (John 19:41). There they placed it on a low shelf carved from the limestone. Their final act of worship was to guide a heavy round stone across the entrance. The Gospel of Matthew tells us Joseph then "went away" (27:60). Joseph and Nicodemus had completed their tender act of devotion.

The silence that followed after the stone at the tomb's entrance ground to its final resting place seemed to echo Christ's earlier proclamation of *"Tetelestai"*—"It is finished!" Even though Jesus's words expressed victory, the women felt only defeat and despair.

The Waiting

Mary Magdalene and Mary the wife of Clopas continued to keep their vigil—only this time they sat across from the tomb. In the last few minutes before the coming of the Sabbath, the two Marys hurried away to purchase spices and ointments for anointing Jesus's body. They made a few purchases before the shops closed and returned through deserted streets to their place of lodging. The Sabbath had arrived.

While others gathered inside homes around the dinner table, the women gathered around work tables to mix spices and oils for anointing—one of the few Sabbath labors allowed by Jewish law. Eventually, a bowl of cool water removed the dust from their faces, hands, and feet, and thin pallets brought relief to their physical exhaustion—but water and pallets could not bring peace to their hearts.

The Guards

Mary Magdalene, Mary the wife of Clopas, Joanna, Salome, Susanna, Mary the mother of Jesus, and her sister rested on the Sabbath in obedience to the law. But while the women rested and waited, the priests spoke with Pilate about securing the tomb. They said, "We remember that while he was still alive that deceiver said, 'After three days I will rise again.' So give the order for the tomb to be made secure until the third day. Otherwise, his disciples may come and steal the body and tell the people that he has been raised from the dead" (Matt. 27:63–64). With Pilate's permission, they posted guards and sealed the large stone to the tomb with cording and wax.

Inactivity of the Sabbath caused the hours to inch by. By the time shops reopened at the Sabbath's end, the women had a plan. Mary Magdalene, Mary the wife of Clopas, and Salome left to find a shop opened for evening sales. There they purchased additional *aromata*, sweet spices in oil, for the next morning's anointing. Then, once more, they waited through the deep darkness of another long night.

Even though Christ had announced that he would rise on the third day, death felt so final—just as it does today. Even though we know that deceased loved ones who know Christ will experience resurrection at Christ's second coming, the separation and waiting make the fulfillment of Christ's promise seem unbearably distant.

7

The Visit to the Tomb

On the first day of the week, very early in the
morning, the women took the spices they had prepared and went to the tomb.

Luke 24:1

On the first day of the week, Mary Magdalene, Mary
the wife of Clopas, Salome, Joanna, and others with
them left for the tomb while it was still dark (Mark 16:1; Luke
24:9–10). They asked each other as they walked, "Who will
roll the stone away from the entrance of the tomb?" (Mark
16:3). They continued on even though they had no answer
for their question. The first morning rays shone in the garden
as they arrived at the tomb.

Angelic Visitations

Matthew—the only Gospel to record the crucifixion earthquake—also records the garden tomb earthquake. "There was a violent earthquake, for an angel of the Lord came down from heaven and, going to the tomb, rolled back the stone and sat on it. His appearance was like lightning, and his clothes were white as snow. The guards were so afraid of him that they shook and became like dead men" (28:2–4).

When the terrified guards scattered, some of the guards went into the city and reported everything to the chief priests. The priests and elders quickly devised a plan and gave the soldiers a large sum of money to say, "His disciples came during the night and stole him away while we were asleep" (Matt. 28:13). The priests and elders also committed to keep the guards out of trouble if the report got to the governor.

Luke records the women's personal encounter with angels at the tomb following the earth's upheaval.[1] "Suddenly two men in clothes that gleamed like lightning stood beside them. In their fright the women bowed down with their faces to the ground, but the men said to them, 'Why do you look for the living among the dead?'" (24:4–5). "Do not be afraid, for I know that you are looking for Jesus, who was crucified" (Matt. 28:5). "'He is not here; he has risen! Remember how he told you, while he was still with you in Galilee: "The Son of Man must be delivered into the hands of sinful men, be crucified and on the third day be raised again."' Then they remembered his words" (Luke 24:6–8). So the women hurried away from the tomb, "afraid yet filled with joy" (Matt. 28:8).

"He Is Risen"

Mary Magdalene, Joanna, Salome, Mary the mother of James, and the others with them hurried to deliver the angels' message to the Eleven and all the others in mourning with them. They faithfully gave their report, but the apostles did not believe them since the women's words "seemed to them like nonsense" (Luke 24:11).[2]

Nevertheless, Peter and John ran to the garden tomb to verify the women's report. John, arriving first, looked in at the strips of linen lying there but did not go in. Simon Peter soon arrived and entered the tomb. He too saw the strips of linen as well as the burial cloth from Jesus's head folded up by itself, separate from the rest. When John stepped inside the tomb with Peter, he "saw and believed" (John 20:8). But Peter returned home, "wondering to himself what had happened" (Luke 24:12).

Christ Appears to Mary Magdalene

The two disciples returned to their homes, but Mary returned to the grave site and remained outside the tomb crying (John 20:13, 15). As she wept, she stooped over to look into the tomb. Two angels dressed in white sat where Jesus's body had been—one at the head and the other at the foot. They asked, "Woman, why are you crying?" (John 20:13).

"They have taken my Lord away," she said, "and I don't know where they have put him" (v. 14). Aware of someone else's presence, Mary turned around.

"Woman," Jesus said, "why are you crying? Who is it you are looking for?" (v. 15).

Thinking he was the gardener, Mary replied, "Sir, if you have carried him away, tell me where you have put him, and I will get him" (v. 15).

Jesus simply spoke her name, "Mary" (v. 16).

Mary's response to recognizing Christ burst forth from a heart full of love and joy, "Rabboni!" (v. 16).[3] She spontaneously prostrated herself before Jesus, clasping his feet, a cultural expression of affection and adoration.

Jesus responded by saying, "Do not hold on to me, for I have not yet returned to the Father. Go instead to my brothers and tell them, 'I am returning to my Father and your Father, to my God and your God'" (v. 17).

In obedience, Mary Magdalene ran to the disciples with the news, "I have seen the Lord!" and told them all what Jesus had said to her (v. 18).

Adam Clarke, an Irish preacher and scholar of the late 1700s, eloquently recorded these thoughts about Mary Magdalene: "Let it be remarked that Mary Magdalene sought Jesus more fervently and continued more affectionately attached to him than any of the rest; therefore, to her first, Jesus is pleased to show himself, and she is made the first herald of the Gospel of a risen Savior."[4]

Christ Appears to the Other Women

Joanna, Salome, Mary the mother of James, and the others with them also encountered the risen Lord upon returning from the garden tomb. Jesus addressed them with the simple word—"Greetings." The women immediately moved closer to him, fell with their faces toward the ground, and clasped his feet in joy and worship. Knowing the turmoil and despair of their hearts, Jesus comforted them with the tender words "Do not be afraid" and commissioned them to deliver a personal message. "Go and tell my brothers to go to Galilee; there they will see me" (Matt. 28:9–10). Once again the women left with Christ's message and the wonderful news of the risen Lord.

Luter and McReynolds write, "The message of Jesus's resurrection is entrusted to the fearful women disciples. What a heavy responsibility! But what better role and at what better time could Jesus have chosen to underline the tremendous significance of the women?"[5]

Christ Appears to the Disciples

Jesus later appeared to others. The Gospel of Mark says that on the same day "Jesus appeared in a different form to two of them while they were walking in the country. These returned and reported it to the rest; but they did not believe them either. Later Jesus appeared to the Eleven as they were eating; he rebuked them for their lack of faith and their stubborn refusal to believe those who had seen him after he had risen" (16:12–14). Christ also appeared to seven disciples on the shores of the Sea of Galilee and to five hundred people in Galilee before eventually ascending from the Mount of Olives to the right hand of the Father in heaven (John 21:1–14; 1 Cor. 15:6; Mark 16:19).

The Wonder of It All

Mary Magdalene, Mary the mother of James, Joanna, Salome, and the others with them surely marveled at the honor of seeing the risen Christ. Imagine their conversations with one another as they reflected on his personal words of greeting, his message "Do not be afraid," and his directive to tell the others. What a privilege! What an affirmation of Christ's love and compassion toward the very ones who had expressed their own love and devotion to him!

Scripture remains silent as to why Jesus waited to reveal himself after Peter and John left the tomb. Gilbert Bilezikian comments, "It was the reward of the loyal female disciples who had accompanied Jesus to the place of crucifixion and stayed with him through the horror of his execution, to be entrusted by him with the most powerful message that has ever impacted the world: 'He is risen.'"[6] Luter and McReynolds add, "They were present at Jesus's lowest point on the cross, and they were honored to be the first witnesses at the resurrection."[7] How they must have marveled at the wonder of it all!

8

Sharing the Good News

God made him who had no sin to be sin for us, so
that in him we might become the righteousness of
God.

2 Corinthians 5:21

The women had wonderful news to tell the disciples—and
tell it they did! After making their initial announcement
of the empty tomb and the angels' message of the resurrected
Christ, they continued repeating the news! Luke uses verb
tenses that effectively communicate to his readers the excite-
ment of the moment. "When they came back from the tomb,
they *told* all these things to the Eleven and to all the others. It
was Mary Magdalene, Joanna, Mary the mother of James and
the others with them who *told* [continued to tell] this to the

apostles" (24:9–10, emphasis added). The exhilaration washed away the exhaustion and replaced despair with hope—even if the disciples didn't believe them!

The women witnessed amazing events—the crucifixion and burial of the Son of God and now the resurrected Savior! The angels reminded them at the tomb of Christ's previous words in Galilee, "The Son of Man must be delivered into the hands of sinful men, be crucified and on the third day be raised again" (Luke 24:7). Luke tells us they did remember—but they had only just begun to understand the significance of all they had seen.

Christ Became Sin

What actually occurred in the spiritual realms as Christ agonized on the cross? The thieves on either side of him suffered too. How was Christ's agony different? What transpired in the heavenly realms beyond what the women could see?

Christ's agony encompassed more than thorns, nails, and lacerations from scourging. His most excruciating agony was emotional and spiritual. During the three hours of darkness from noon until 3:00, God turned his back in full rejection, because "God made him who had no sin to be sin for us" (2 Cor. 5:21).

Imagine every hideous and vile deed committed from the beginning of time until Christ's future return—heaped upon the pure and perfect Son of God. Bearing the sin of many, he drank the very cup of wrath he prayed would be taken from him. No other pain can compare to Christ's separation from his Father.

"In that moment of time the finite and infinite [united], and the Son of God paid in full a penalty imposed for the sin of every human being from Adam to history's end. . . . He had suffered more than all our race together and He suffered there for you and me."[1]

Christ Became Our Sacrificial Lamb

The Passover feast reveals the significance of the symbolism of Christ's sacrificial death as the Lamb of God. In preparation for the annual Passover meal, more than 18,000 Jewish men passed through the congested temple court. Each man carried a lamb draped across his shoulders, a one-year-old unblemished male.

A priest collected the lamb's blood for an offering, but the lamb itself was roasted for the evening Passover meal—the same last meal the Lord shared with his disciples. Symbolically and literally, Jesus became our sacrificial Passover Lamb. "As his death was unique, so also his anguish; and our best response to it is hushed worship."[2]

In the final years of his life, John the apostle wrote in Revelation about Christ—the Lamb of God. John described the Lamb in his vision of heaven: "Then I looked and heard the voice of many angels, numbering thousands upon thousands, and ten thousand times ten thousand. . . . In a loud voice they sang: 'Worthy is the Lamb, who was slain, to receive power and wealth and wisdom and strength and honor and glory and praise!'" (5:11–12). One day all believers will see him and join with the angels in singing for eternity, "Worthy is the Lamb. . . ."

Christ Provided a New Relationship with God

Christ's death not only satisfied the holiness and righteousness of God, it also made a way for believers to come boldly and confidently into God's presence—as his own adopted children. God portrayed this new relationship to the priests in the temple when Christ died. At the moment of his death, the temple curtain ripped from top to bottom—as if by the hand of God. The temple curtain provided a visual separation between a holy God, represented by the Holy of Holies, and sinful humanity. Christ's death allowed believers to come right into God's presence with no barriers of sin, guilt, or shame.

The apostle Paul explained this new relationship when he wrote, "In him and through faith in him we may approach God with freedom and confidence" (Eph. 3:12). Christ's atonement for sin restored our broken relationship between God and humankind. Through God's sacrifice that canceled our sins, he reinstates us to a relationship of "at-one-ment" with God. John wrote the wonderful news, "He is the atoning sacrifice for our sins, and not only for ours but also for the sins of the whole world" (1 John 2:2).

Christ's death also allows believers to relate to God the Father with personal intimacy. With the faith of a child, believers can cry out, "*Abba*, Father"—Daddy. Paul provides a beautiful summary of this new relationship: "When the time had fully come, God sent his Son, born of a woman, born under law, to redeem those under law, that we might receive the full rights of sons. Because you are sons, God sent the Spirit of his Son into our hearts, the Spirit who calls out, '*Abba*, Father'" (Gal. 4:4–6).

Christ Provided Victory over Sin

Christ's death broke the power of sin. Followers of Christ could now experience freedom from sins that formerly controlled their lives. They no longer had to live as "slaves to sin" (Rom. 6:6). Although they could follow the prompting of sin, sin would not regain the domination and control it had before conversion.

When followers of Christ identify their sin-prone nature with the death of Christ, they choose to count themselves dead to sin but alive to God in Christ Jesus—free to obey him and live for him. Believers are free to rejoice and proclaim with Paul, "Through Christ Jesus the law of the Spirit of life set me free from the law of sin and death" (Rom. 8:2).

Christ Provided Victory over Death

Death entered the world with sin in the Garden of Eden. Paul wrote about Christ's victory over death in a letter to the believers in Corinth. "'Death has been swallowed up in victory. Where, O death, is your victory? Where, O death, is your sting?' . . . But thanks be to God! He gives us the victory through our Lord Jesus Christ" (1 Cor. 15:54–57).

The author of the Letter to the Hebrews also emphasized this wonderful victory. "Since the children have flesh and blood, he too shared in their humanity so that by his death he might destroy him who holds the power of death—that is, the devil—and free those who all their lives were held in slavery by their fear of death" (2:14–15).

69

Christ Provided Eternal Life

Christ's resurrection overcame the powers of evil and death (1 Cor. 15:12–19).[3] Christ experienced death so that we would not have to. Even though our physical body will one day die, our spiritual self will never die. One of the most well-known verses of Scripture, John 3:16, communicates this profound truth: "For God so loved the world that he gave his one and only Son, that whoever believes in him shall not perish but have eternal life."

The apostle John wrote that those totally committed to Jesus Christ begin to experience the blessings of eternal life through knowing God while still here on earth. Death simply provides the fullest expression of knowing Christ.[4] Paul said in 1 Corinthians 13:12, "Now we see but a poor reflection as in a mirror; then we shall see face to face. Now I know in part; then I shall know fully, even as I am fully known." Christ's prayer following that last Passover meal with the disciples communicated this. "Now this is eternal life: that they may know you, the only true God, and Jesus Christ, whom you have sent" (John 17:2–3).

Oswald Chambers eloquently wrote, "The only ground on which God can forgive us is the tremendous tragedy of the Cross of Christ. . . . Forgiveness which is so easy for us to accept, cost the agony of Calvary. When once you realize all that it cost God to forgive you, you will be held as in a vice, constrained by the love of God."[5]

Continuing to Share the News

The women shared a simple but profound message: "I have seen the Lord!" (John 20:18). Christ had risen! But within that message was much more to discover and joyfully experience. Christ living within the believer, victory over sin through the power of the Holy Spirit, adoption into God's family, victory over death, and eternal life with Christ were deep truths to learn, apply, and share. Women continue to delve into the depths of this amazing good news today—and continue to share it. Despite sacrifice and hardship, they remain faithful to proclaim, "He is risen! Come and see!"

PART 3

WOMEN DRAWN TO THE CROSS THROUGH THE AGES

Discover the stories of faithful women who served Christ during the earliest years of the Christian church as well as the centuries that followed. Grieve and rejoice for women who willingly gave their lives or faced persecution for their devotion to Christ.

Observe how women ministered through their homes or influenced lives by sharing their resources. See how their passion to share Christ's salvation and the truth of his Word continues to impact the world today.

9

Women Who Served
through Suffering

Join with me in suffering for the gospel, by the
power of God, who has saved us and called us to a
holy life.

2 Timothy 1:8–9

Women, as well as men, have shared in the sufferings
of Christ throughout the last two thousand years.
For some, such as Vibia Perpetua and Ann Judson, it meant
giving their lives. Catherine of Siena endured the physical
hardships and deprivation of serving the dying and destitute. Regardless of the cost, they rejoiced at the privilege
of sharing the sufferings of their beloved Christ. These

women and scores like them, many whose names are lost to us, call us to deepen our commitment to give whatever Christ requires of us.

Vibia Perpetua—An Early Martyr

Christians from Rome took their faith south across the Mediterranean Sea to the shores of North Africa where they established vibrant churches. Roman persecution soon followed. Vibia Perpetua, a young girl from the North African city of Carthage, documented her story of martyrdom from her conversion and arrest up to the day of her execution in March of AD 203.

Perpetua had many reasons to deny her newfound faith—nobility, education, youth, and a young infant. She recorded the following shortly after her arrest along with Felicitas, her maidservant; her teacher; and three fellow believers. She wrote while they waited in the dungeon for their sentencing, "I was very much afraid because I had never experienced such gloom. O terrible day! Fearful heat because of the crowd and from the jostling of the soldiers! Finally I was racked with anxiety for my infant."[1]

When two church deacons arranged for her infant to be brought to her in prison, she wrote, "I suckled my child, who was already weak from want of nourishment. . . . I then obtained leave that my child should remain with me in the prison. Immediately I gained strength and being relieved from my anxiety about the child, my prison suddenly became to me a palace, so that I preferred to be there rather than anywhere else."[2]

While standing before the tribunal for her sentencing, Perpetua announced, "I cannot forsake my faith for freedom." The governor passed sentence on all of them—the torture of wild beasts in the arena, then death by a gladiator's sword. Perpetua wrote, "We returned to prison in high spirits."[3]

Perpetua's journal then focused attention on her maidservant, Felicitas, eight months pregnant. Since Romans did not publicly punish an expectant woman, Felicitas worried she would not face death with her Christian friends but die alone after the birth of her child.

Three days before their execution date, Perpetua and her friends prayed that Felicitas would deliver her baby. God answered their prayers. That night labor pains began and Felicitas gave birth to a healthy daughter to be raised by her sister. With the heart of a mother, Perpetua wrote this tender notation after seeing her own infant for the last time: "God so ordered it that it [the child] was no longer required to suck, nor did my milk inconvenience me."[4]

On execution day, Perpetua led the way with a calm, radiant face and a song on her lips. She remembered how the apostle Paul witnessed Stephen's stoning and became a believer shortly afterward. She prayed that those in the arena who witnessed her death would also come to know her Christ.

Guards stripped Perpetua and Felicitas of their clothes and displayed them in a net in the arena. When the crowd protested over seeing "one young woman of delicate frame, and another with breasts still dripping from her recent childbirth,"[5] the Romans responded by providing tunics to cover their bodies.

After a fierce cow gored her, Perpetua stood up and went to comfort Felicitas, who had also been tossed by the cow. As

77

they stood together ready for another charge, the spectators shouted "Enough!" and called for the gladiator. The trembling gladiator ineptly gave Perpetua only slight wounds. After a cry of pain, she "placed the wavering right hand of the youthful gladiator to her throat" and died.[6]

Because of Perpetua's and her companions' courageous faith, the church grew. The new converts wanted to know the God who produced such heroines and heroes. Perpetua spoke her last recorded words to the guards at the coliseum's gate. These same words offer comfort today as we read, with difficulty, Perpetua's testimony. She seemed to identify with Christ's own heart at the cross. "Stand fast in the faith, and love one another, all of you, and so not be offended at my sufferings."[7]

Tertullian, an early church father, added the following postscript to her life, "O most brave and blessed martyrs! O truly called and chosen unto the glory of our Lord Jesus Christ!"[8]

Catherine of Siena—Lay Worker and Activist for Church Reform, 1347–1380

Catherine Benincasa lived in the Italian city of Siena and ministered as a laywoman in an age when the church limited a woman's religious work to the confines of a convent.[9] Even though she lacked education, wealth, and social standing, she possessed enormous devotion and courage.

Catherine pleaded with the rich and poor, sick and healthy to acknowledge their need of Christ. She entered prisons and attended public executions to comfort the accused with her prayers and songs. Christ's radiance shone through her in the dark world of injustice and brutality in medieval Italy. Catherine expressed her love for Christ as she cared for those dying from cancer and leprosy. She believed these experiences helped her share in the suffering of the crucified Christ.

In 1374 the black death struck Siena and more than 80,000 died—one-third of the city's population. While others fled, Catherine and her assistants stayed in the city and worked tirelessly day and night to care for the sick and dying.

After the black death subsided, Catherine addressed the corruption in the church. She spent four to six hours a day in prayer for the restoration and purification of the church. She also made personal visits and wrote fiery letters to the pope.

Along with her benevolent work and church reform, Catherine found time to write. Shortly before her death, she dictated her most famous work, *The Dialogue*.[10] Catherine's twenty-six prayers comprised a second volume. Nearly four hundred letters addressed to kings, popes, political corporations, and individuals formed a third volume. Even though Catherine died at age thirty-three, she influenced the city of Siena and papal leadership with the strength and love she found in Christ.

Ann Judson—Wife of America's First Foreign Missionary, 1789–1826

Ann Judson, the most noted of the early missionary wives, provided a role model for Christian young women responding to God's call. Ann began seeking God in Bible study and prayer as a teenager. She composed a prayer reflecting her desire to serve Christ with her life: "Direct me in Thy service, and I ask no more. I would not choose my position of work, or place of labor. Only let me know Thy will, and I will readily comply."[11]

Both Adoniram Judson, Ann's suitor, and Ann felt a call to missions in India. Her commission contained the wording "call to ministry" at a time when women's assignments in missionary work focused on maintaining the home and raising children.

In spite of difficult living conditions and illness, Ann came to love Burma, where she learned about the Lord's mercy and grace. When war broke out between Britain and Burma in 1823, the Burmese government considered all Americans associates of the British. They threw Adoniram into a death prison, and Ann, two months pregnant, lived as a prisoner in the inner room of her own house. She valiantly pled with government officials for Adoniram's life for two years while secretly bringing supplies and food to him and his fellow prisoners.[12]

Ann wrote about that time, "My prevailing opinion was, that my husband would suffer violent death; and that I should, of course, become a slave. . . . But the consolations of religion, in these trying circumstances, were neither 'few nor small!' It taught me to look beyond this world, to that rest . . . where Jesus reigns and oppression never enters."[13]

Inspirational writing and gripping stories of struggles and life on the mission field serve as some of Ann's greatest contributions. Letters home made the Judsons' adventures so vivid in the minds of Americans that the Judson name became practically a household word. Ann wrote heartrending accounts of child marriages, female infanticide, and the burdens of the Burmese women under the "tyrannic rod" of their husbands. Her concern even moved past the Burmese women's ill-treatment to their isolation and lack of instruction.

Appeals from Ann arrived in America, exhorting women to join with her in improving the lives of the Burmese women. "Shall we, my beloved friends, suffer minds like these to lie dormant, to wither in ignorance and delusion, to grope their way to eternal ruin, without an effort on our part, to raise, to refine, to elevate, and point to that Savior who has died equally for them as for us? . . . Let us make a united effort, let us call on all, old and young, . . . to instruct, to enlighten and to save females in the Eastern world."[14]

Ann served for thirteen years in Burma until her impoverished death. As the first woman missionary to leave America, Ann's story of constant love for Christ encouraged many other women to serve on the mission field. Ann's willingness to obey despite the hardships reflected the heart of the women who traveled and served Christ. She understood Christ's admonition concerning ministry, "Whatever you did for one of the least of these brothers of mine, you did for me" (Matt. 25:40).

10

Women Who Opened Their Homes

Aquila and Priscilla greet you warmly in the Lord,
and so does the church that meets at their home.

1 Corinthians 16:19

The home has formed the heart of the church from the first days of Christianity in Jerusalem to the current house churches of China. When women make their homes available for worship and Bible study, lives are changed. Priscilla, Marcella, Katherine von Bora, and Susanna Wesley offer examples of a woman's godly influence through her home.

Priscilla—Leader in the Early Church

For the first three hundred years of the church, house churches were the norm. At the heart of this early movement, we find Prisca, or Priscilla. Paul's letter to the church in Rome and his letter to Timothy both include a warm personal greeting to Priscilla and her husband, Aquila. In addition, Paul includes in his letter to the Corinthian church a personal greeting from Aquila and Priscilla as well as a greeting from the church that met in their house.

Scripture never mentions Priscilla apart from her husband. But four of the six New Testament references list Priscilla first.[1] In the first century, good Greek syntax used the name of the most prominent person first—emphasizing that person's position or social status. Some think Aquila, possibly a freed Roman slave, had a lower social status than Priscilla. Others believe Priscilla's prominence in the church brought her the distinction of being named first.[2]

Aquila and Priscilla settled in Corinth in AD 49, after the emperor expelled all Jews from Rome. They took their faith as well as their tent-making skills with them. Paul stayed in their home and made tents along with them when he visited Corinth.

From the first mention in Scripture to the last, Priscilla and Aquila kept an open heart and an open door. The long hours at their craft allowed plenty of time to visit. Imagine the rich conversations they must have shared around the work tables by day and the dinner table at night!

Paul loved his two friends to the end of his earthly life, mentioning them often in his letters. Just before he was beheaded by Nero in Rome, he sent his greeting to Priscilla, showing his deep and affectionate love and respect for his dear sister in Christ by using her familiar name, Prisca.[3]

After Claudius died, Priscilla and Aquila returned to Rome, yet we last hear of them in Ephesus once again. Wherever we find this husband and wife ministry team, we see their home as a center of Christian service "radiating friendship, fellowship, and love."[4]

Marcella—A Woman of Influence

Marcella lived a luxurious life in Rome. After her conversion, she turned her palatial home into a Christian retreat for Bible studies and ministry to the poor. She often invited famous leaders of the church to teach there. In AD 382 she invited Jerome, a renowned scholar working on a Latin translation of the Scriptures.[5]

Jerome frequently discussed the Scriptures with Marcella while visiting in her home. He expressed amazement that she was able to learn on her own what he learned from "diligent study and meditation." Jerome wrote, "Her delight in the Scriptures was incredible. She was forever singing, 'Thy word have I hid in mine heart that I might not sin against thee'" (Ps. 119:11).

Marcella's devotion influenced a large circle of aristocratic and influential Roman women desiring to follow Christ in obedience and devotion.

Katherine von Bora—Wife of Martin Luther, 1499–1552

In 1517 Martin Luther, a professor at the University of Wittenberg in Germany, posted his famous list of Ninety-five Theses, which created instant outrage and brought him into prominence overnight. He proposed a discussion of the Roman Catholic Church's sale of indulgences—a payment of money absolving the purchaser of his or her sin.[6]

Behind the doors of a convent, Katherine von Bora launched her own protest. Katherine's discontent continued to increase with the convent's rules of silence and limited visiting among the nuns. She eventually escaped, along with ten other nuns—a crime worthy of death. The plot entailed a herring merchant who delivered ten barrels of herring and exited with ten barrels of nuns!

Martin Luther assisted some of the nuns in finding a home, employment, or a husband. Katherine, declining the gentleman selected for her, sent word she would consider either Dr. Amsdorf, one of Luther's staff, or Luther himself. Luther wrote in a letter to his friends, "While I was thinking of other things, God has suddenly brought me to marriage. . . . God likes to work miracles!"[7]

After Katherine and Martin married, she moved into his home, the former Augustinian monastery at Wittenberg. She immediately focused on cleaning the huge building and bringing order to Luther's daily life. Luther commented, "There's a lot to get used to in the first year of marriage. One wakes up in the morning and finds a pair of pigtails on the pillow which were not there before!"[8]

Katherine worked hard by Luther's side raising six children and four orphans. She looked after the parsonage and tended the orchards, gardens, fishpond, and barnyard animals—even butchering the stock herself.[9] In addition, Katherine graciously hosted the hundreds of students or guests passing through the Luther home. Luther called her "the morning star of Wittenberg," because she awakened at 4:00 a.m. to tend to her many responsibilities.

Martin Luther admired and appreciated his "Katie," saying, "This life has nothing more lovely and delightful than a woman who loves her husband."[10] He publicly thanked God for his "pious and true wife on whom a husband's heart can rely."[11]

Even though two of their children died, Katherine experienced her greatest loss at Luther's death—after twenty-one years of marriage. When armies invaded Wittenberg, she retreated twice with her children to other towns for safety. She returned each time to rebuild her barns and sheds, replace the cattle, and replant the garden destroyed by the soldiers. But then bubonic plague forced her to leave the city with her children once again.

Katherine von Bora Luther served Christ every season of her life—as a single woman, a wife, and a widow. She continued to respond to issues and needs around her with courage, compassion, and grace, as demonstrated by her Lord on the cross.

Susanna Wesley—Christian Mother and Teacher of God's Word, 1669–1742

God worked through the personalities and conflicted marriage of Susanna and Samuel Wesley, an Anglican priest serving at Epworth in Lincolnshire, England, even though their difference of opinions in practical and political issues continued throughout their married life.[12]

Susanna Wesley gave birth to nineteen children, with ten surviving. The frequent absences of Samuel on church business left management of the home in her hands. Through hard days of caring for ten children alone, she remained steadfast, teaching God's Word by her example of daily trust. She once wrote: "We must know God experientially for unless the heart perceive and know him to be the supreme good, her only happiness . . . unless the soul feel and acknowledge that, she can have no repose, no peace, no joy, but in loving and being loved by him."[13]

In 1703, during a period of reconciliation with her husband, Susanna conceived John Wesley. Later, during a tragic house fire, John barely escaped alive. Susanna told God, "I intend to be more particularly careful of the soul of this child . . . that I may do my endeavors to instill into his mind the disciplines of Thy true religion and virtue."[14]

Just like Salome, the mother of the apostles James and John, Susanna raised two sons who influenced the world with the message of salvation through Christ. John Wesley, along with Charles, profoundly impacted the evangelical revival in Britain through preaching, writing, and composing hymns.[15]

Priscilla, Marcella, Katherine von Bora Luther, and Susanna Wesley stand among the ranks of faithful women. They responded as the women at the cross—by listening and learning from the words of Christ. They continue to touch lives as their legacies model courageous commitment to their Savior.

11

Women Who Influenced through Their Resources

If anyone gives even a cup of cold water to one of these little ones because he is my disciple, I tell you the truth, he will certainly not lose his reward.

Matthew 10:42

Women throughout the ages have offered their resources for Christ's work, just like the women who supported Jesus's ministry. Some, like Paula and Emily Tubman, invested their finances. Isabella of Castile used her political influence, while others like Vittoria Colonna influenced through passion for the message of Christ's love.

Paula—Financially Supported Jerome's Translation of the Vulgate

Paula lived extravagantly in a gilded palace in Rome. Her wealth, however, failed to protect her from grief and loss when her husband died and left her with five young children.

In an attempt to find comfort, Paula attended Jerome's Bible lectures at the home of her friend Marcella. Through these lectures, Paula not only came to know Christ as her Lord, but she also developed a deep friendship with Jerome, the gifted teacher.

As Jerome prepared to return to his home in the Holy Land, he persuaded Paula to come see where Christ lived and died. Paula responded to the extreme poverty she found there by financing five houses serving needs of the destitute.

Paula also continued assisting Jerome in his translation of the Bible by personally purchasing ancient books and rare manuscripts as well as by providing assistants to copy manuscripts.

Jerome dedicated his Latin translations of Job, Isaiah, Samuel, Kings, Esther, Galatians, Philemon, Titus, and the twelve Minor Prophets to Paula and her oldest daughter, Eustochium, who worked alongside her. Jerome commented when criticized for dedicating his work to women:

> There are people, O Paula and Eustochium, who take offense at seeing your names at the beginning of my works. These people do not know that while Barak trembled, Deborah saved Israel; that Esther delivered from supreme peril the children of God. I passed over in silence Anna and Elizabeth and the other holy women of the Gospel—but humble stars compared with the luminary, Mary. Is it not to women that our Lord

appeared after his Resurrection? Yes, and the men could then blush for not having sought what women had found.[1]

Paula never returned to Rome and died in Bethlehem in AD 404. Jerome explained in a letter that as she lay dying, "it seemed as though she were leaving strangers to go home to her own people."[2]

Isabella of Castile—Founded the First Christian Church in the New World, 1451–1504

Prayer sustained Isabella throughout her life, including her career as queen of Castile—the largest of the Spanish kingdoms and a leading power in Europe. At her coronation, she left the ceremony and walked immediately to the cathedral. Humbly calling herself a handmaiden of the Lord, she gave thanks to God for bringing her safely through so many perils to such a high honor. She asked for grace to rule according to God's will and to use the authority he had given her with justice and wisdom.

Isabella provided strong spiritual, political, and military leadership and led Spain into one of the most memorable epochs in its history. She abolished the bribing of officials and set up courts of justice, hearing doubtful cases and appeals herself.

The great explorer Columbus appeared in her court for the first time in 1484, asking for money for a voyage to the New World. She listened attentively as he explained how his plan would advance Christendom. She also carefully noted his biblical response to church leaders who believed the earth was flat.

Isabella and her husband, Ferdinand, eventually gave permission in 1492 for Columbus to sail—with the aim of taking Christianity to the New World. On his second voyage in 1493, Queen Isabella sent clergymen for the first Christian church in the New World. They built the church in a town named after the queen in what is now the Dominican Republic.

In addition to military and political leadership, Queen Isabella influenced growth of universities, hospitals, and churches. She also established printing presses—publishing the first multilanguage Bible, the *Complutensian Polyglot*. It contained the Hebrew Old Testament, the Greek Septuagint, the Latin Vulgate, the Greek New Testament, and the first five Old Testament books in Aramaic.

One of the world's greatest Christian rulers, Isabella died at age fifty-three—two weeks before Columbus returned from his fourth and last voyage. Upon hearing of her death, Columbus wrote, "We may rest assured that she is received in His Glory, and beyond the care of this rough and weary world."[3]

Vittoria Colonna—Michelangelo's Inspiration, 1490–1547

Vittoria Colonna chose a pure and gracious life even though surrounded by the extravagance and immorality of Renaissance Rome. She refused many offers of marriage as one of the most beautiful and celebrated widows in Italy. She turned instead to her faith for solace until it became her one absorbing love.

During the early years of her life, Vittoria enjoyed affluence and luxuries, including an ornate castle on Ischia, an island off the coast of Italy. Yet, toward the end of her life, she preferred the simple lifestyle of a convent.

Vittoria Colonna probably met Michelangelo in Rome ten years after the death of her husband. Their first recorded meeting took place in 1538—he was sixty-three years old and she, forty-seven. Vittoria stood on occasion and watched as Michelangelo painted "The Last Judgment" behind the altar in the Sistine Chapel, the pope's private chapel.

The growing friendship strengthened their faith and enriched their lives. The great painter brought friendship and loving understanding into Vittoria's life. She in turn inspired and encouraged the aging artist in his grand endeavors. They also shared the same longing for a purified church. Each worked in his or her own way for reform, he with his brush, she with her pen.

In letters exchanged between Michelangelo and Vittoria, we witness an encounter with the crucifixion of Christ. When he sent sketches of his drawing entitled *Crucifixion* to Vittoria, she replied, "I have received your letter and examined the 'Crucifixion.' . . . Nowhere could one find another figure of our Lord so well executed, so lovingly and so exquisitely finished."[4]

When she received a second drawing by mail, she replied, "I had the greatest faith in God that he would bestow upon you supernatural grace for the making of this Christ, and when I saw it, it was so wonderful that it surpassed all my expectations in every way."[5]

During the final hour of her life, Vittoria requested that Michelangelo read a prayer from her personal writings portraying her desire to ascend to heaven. "I beseech Thee, most tender Father, that Thy most living fire may purify me, that

Thy most clear light may illumine me, and that Thy most pure love may so avail me that, without hindrance of mortal things, I may return to Thee in happiness and security."[6]

Vittoria Colonna's humble spirit continued to the very end of her life. At her request, neither a stone nor tablet marks her grave.

Emily H. Tubman—Called to Financial Stewardship, 1794–1885

Emily Thomas met and married Richard Tubman, a wealthy southern planter and exporter, in Augusta, Georgia. After eighteen years of marriage, Richard died. His will requested that Emily apply to the Georgia legislature for passage of a law allowing her to free their slaves. This radical request came twenty-six years before Lincoln's Emancipation Proclamation of 1862.

Emily had shared Christ's freedom from sin with her slaves, and now she sought to offer literal freedom as well. During the legal process, Emily found guidance and encouragement in the apostle Paul's statement, "There is neither Jew nor Greek, slave nor free, male nor female, for you are all one in Christ Jesus" (Gal. 3:28).

Sixty-nine of the freed Tubman slaves chose to return to the West African republic of Liberia. Seventy-five others remained with Mrs. Tubman. To these she gave land, clothing, and regular provisions until they acquired self-sufficiency.

The other freed slaves set sail on a chartered ship arriving at Harper, Liberia. Emily contributed generously to a fund in Liberia for homes and supplies for her own freed slaves as well as for others arriving from the United States. Tubman-town, a city named in her honor, acknowledged her vision and generosity.

In the following years, Emily clung to her faith as the battles of the Civil War came nearer Augusta. When General William Sherman of the Union Army marched on Georgia, she wrote in one of her letters, "The Book of books not only comforts us here under the various trials and bereavements of life, but by diligent study of its divine teachings, educates and prepares us for the enjoyment of the highest and more holy society of heaven."[7]

Fortunately, most of Emily's land, bank, and bond investments survived the war years. At the close of the war, she and other stockholders of the Georgia Railroad provided free transportation home to weary Confederate soldiers. In addition, she fed and clothed numerous families of husbands killed in the war.

Just like Christians in the early church, Emily Tubman shared with those in need. She believed, "I am a steward of the Lord and only hold this money in trust, and my supreme joy is to dispense it to advance His Kingdom or to relieve human suffering."[8]

In her later years, Emily also gave lavishly to Christian colleges, churches, and Christian charities. She discovered the truth of Christ's teaching, "It is more blessed to give than to receive" (Acts 20:35). When Emily Tubman died at age ninety-one, her minister said, "I should say, like Stephen—she was full of faith and good works."[9]

Influential women such as Paula, Vittoria Colonna, Isabella of Castile, and Emily Tubman stand with distinction among faithful women. They responded with their lives and their possessions, just as the women at the cross did. They continue to influence lives today as their legacies model self-sacrifice and devotion to Jesus Christ. They encourage us to be generous with our time and money as we too follow Christ.

12

Women Who Instructed
and Encouraged

> . . . teaching them to obey everything I have com-
> manded you.
>
> Matthew 28:20

A love for God's written Word motivated women such as
Hilda, Hannah Moore, and Pandita Ramabai to invest
their lives teaching God's truths. Others, like Amanda Smith,
spent their lives powerfully communicating the eternal message of God's love and salvation.

Hilda—"All Who Knew Her Called Her Mother,"
614–680

Hilda's life spans an eventful epoch in the early history of
Christianity in England. Hilda formed the head and heart

of a Christian monastery in northeast England—Whitby of Yorkshire. Whitby stood like a beacon on a rocky point three hundred feet above the North Sea.

For more than two decades, Hilda ruled as administrator, teacher, and nurturing spiritual guide to both fishermen and kings alike. We mostly remember her, though, for all she accomplished during the years she spent at Whitby, where she assisted the sick and the poor, brought education to the ignorant, and brought new faith to the weary.

One source of Hilda's revered status comes from fostering the giftedness of a young serf named Caedmon. While lying in the straw of an ox's crib, Caedmon began to sing the story of creation in simple verse. When Hilda heard about the song "birthed in an ox's crib," she brought Caedmon into the monastery to learn more Bible stories. With Hilda's encouragement, Caedmon used his voice, his harp, and short lines of beautiful Celtic-Saxon verse to communicate Old Testament stories as well as the resurrection, ascension, and second coming of Christ to commoners.

Bede—a historian, theologian,[1] and personal acquaintance of Hilda—affectionately tells of her life in his *Ecclesiastical History of the English Nation*. He writes, "All who knew her called her mother, on account of her piety and grace. . . . She never failed to return thanks to her maker or . . . to instruct the flock committed to her charge."[2]

Hannah Moore—English Author and Teacher of Children, 1745–1833

Hannah Moore moved among the prominent persons of London as a gifted playwright. At age thirty-five, she met a group of influential Anglican evangelicals who believed Christians should live out their faith by making a social impact on society. Through these contacts, Hannah had an opportunity to visit the Mendips, a mining area in southwest England.

Hannah responded compassionately to the poverty and ignorance in camp by beginning a school on Sundays. The children learned about the Bible as they learned to read. Most of the textbooks came from Hannah's personal writing skills.

Along with other female leaders of Sunday school work in England, Hannah suffered persecution from the curates in the Church of England. She never let the condemnation deter her and eventually helped organize schools accommodating more than twenty thousand children.

After Hannah's death, her will distributed income from her lifetime of writing to seventy different Christian organizations. She wanted Christian education to continue to influence students' lives. She used her love of the written word to support others as they continued to proclaim God's love—the very love Christ demonstrated on the cross that had transformed her own life. Hannah's life encourages our own faithful stewardship both in life and in death.

Amanda Smith—"God's Image Carved in Ebony," 1837–1915

Amanda Smith, born into slavery in 1837, watched her father work in a broom factory during the day and in the fields harvesting crops during the evenings until he saved enough to purchase the family's freedom. Even though she attended school only a total of three months, she persevered with her mother's help. Amanda learned to read by cutting out large letters from newspapers, laying them on the windowsill, and getting her mother to form them into words.

In 1855, during a service in New York's old Green Street Methodist Episcopal Church, Amanda made an unconditional surrender to God. She soon began earnestly proclaiming God's love and salvation at every opportunity.

In addition to sharing her faith, Amanda prayed through ongoing hardships as well as times of worship. Her richest blessings and stirring revelations of God came while she bent over the washtub or sweated over the ironing table. Other times she would kneel beside an old trunk or under an apple tree—calling her spontaneous prayer time "going the knee route."

In 1876 Amanda received an invitation to evangelize in England. She responded much like the women who traveled with Jesus—willingly leaving the comfort and familiarity of their homes. For almost two years, she participated in evangelistic services all over England and Scotland. Afterward she spent nineteen months evangelizing in Bombay and other major cities in India.

Before returning to the States, Amanda also visited Liberia, West Africa. She stirred many hearts with her message of God's grace in the village of Tubmantown—named after Emily Tubman, the Christian supporter of freed slaves.

Once home in America, she founded and directed the Amanda Smith Orphan's Home for Colored Children in a suburb of Chicago. Just like Mary Magdalene, Joanna, and Susanna, Jesus Christ brought Amanda from a life of despair to one filled with hope. At her death, a minister and friend affectionately described her as "God's image carved in ebony."[3]

Pandita Ramabai—Christian Educator in India, 1858–1922

Christians in India remember Pandita Ramabai as one of their most famous Christian leaders. Her father, a Brahmin priest and wandering guru, traveled with his family from shrines to sacred sites, hoping to appease the gods and find inner peace.

Even though his family lived a life of hardship and deprivation, Ramabai's father insisted she learn to read and write Sanskrit, the Indian language used in literature. Before she was twenty, Ramabai could speak five languages and quote 18,000 verses of the *Purana*, the Sanskrit sacred writings.

Ramabai's father, mother, and older sister eventually died of starvation and exposure from their wanderings. With her brother at her side, Ramabai continued the pilgrimages. They struggled with hunger, doubt, and a thirst for truth. They often fell asleep with empty stomachs in the cold, burying themselves in the sand for warmth. She later wrote, "After years of fruitless service, we began to lose our faith in the Hindu gods."[4] Ramabai and her brother finally ended their quest and settled in Calcutta.

Ramabai continued to study Hindu sacred writings in Calcutta. Scholars there were astonished at her knowledge and named her "Pandita," meaning "learned." While living and studying in Calcutta, she also heard of Christianity and began comparing the Christian and Hindu scriptures.

Pandita Ramabai visited England in 1883 and noticed a tremendous difference in the treatment of women in the Christian faith of the Anglican Church and Hinduism. She realized after reading John 4 that Christ truly was the divine

Savior he claimed to be, and he was the only one who could transform and uplift the downtrodden women of India. She wrote, "While the old Hindu scriptures have given us some beautiful precepts of loving, the new dispensation of Christ has given us grace to carry these principles into practice, and that makes all the difference in the world."[5]

Pandita found her greatest passion in addressing the needs of young widows in India. She eventually turned a family farm into a women's refuge called Mukti, meaning "Salvation." The mission sponsored a school and home for widows, orphans, and illegitimate children. It later expanded to include care of unwanted babies, training of the blind, and ministry to persons with disabilities. In response to the famine in 1896, Pandita brought six hundred starving widows and children back to the safety of Mukti.

In addition to her work with women, Pandita spent the last fifteen years of her life translating the Bible into Mahrathi, a regional Indian language. Though many women have worked on translations of the Scriptures, this work remains the first complete translation by a woman.

Pandita ended her lifelong pilgrimage of seeking the truth when she found the Son of the One True God. She discovered, just like Susanna, Joanna, and Mary Magdalene, the fulfillment and immeasurable joy of a life set free. God's personal love transformed her life, and she in turn uncovered a lifelong passion of sharing that relationship with others.

PART 4

WOMEN AT THE CROSS TODAY

D iscover how the lineage of faithful women continues right up into the twenty-first century as women join in Christ's great work. Examine how we too can worship at the foot of the cross and live a life of devotion and faithfulness, just as the women before us.

13

Women of the Twenty-first Century

> One generation will commend your works to another; they will tell of your mighty acts.
>
> Psalm 145:4

Though externals of the modern world bear little resemblance to the first century, the hearts of women committed to Jesus Christ remain much the same. They still respond with deep emotion to the cross. They look upon Christ's agony and feel his sacrificial love. They also minister under his leadership and learn from him through studying his Word under the leadership of the Holy Spirit.

Christian women also personally know this living Savior who acknowledges their presence and notes their sacrificial acts of adoration and service. This same Jesus continues to affirm women—joining in their laughter and embracing their tears. At the same time, he draws their hearts to seek and to know the one true God.

Christian Women of the Twenty-first Century

Educational opportunities, convenience of travel, electronic communication, and cultural freedoms have opened new doors for many Christian women. A sampling of influential Christian women of the twenty-first century[1] would include Vonette Bright—wife of the late Dr. Bill Bright and initiator of the National Day of Prayer in America; Shirley Dobson—author and wife of Dr. James Dobson; Ruth Bell Graham—author, poet, and wife of evangelist Billy Graham; Kay Arthur, Beth Moore, and Anne Graham Lotz—internationally known Bible teachers and authors; and Joni Eareckson Tada—artist, author, speaker, and activist for disability awareness.

Can you see your name on that list of Christian women? God can! Just like the women at the cross and those drawn to the cross throughout history, each of these women wanted to know Christ's heart. They served him in their individual areas of influence and walked through doors of opportunity as God opened them. Holding nothing back, they gave everything. Even if your name never ends up on a published list of famous women of faith, your name is forever written on the palm of God's hand and on the hearts of those your life touches for Christ.

Power of the Holy Spirit

Today's faithful women also possess unique differences from the women at the crucifixion. The indwelling Holy Spirit plays an active part in how Christians experience the crucifixion. On the day Jesus died, the women stood there in their own power. The sheer strength of their belief and love saw them through the difficult hours. Only after Christ's ascension and the coming of the Holy Spirit at Pentecost did they know his power within.

The Holy Spirit continues to teach, lead, and empower women. He is the Counselor whom Jesus sent to us from the Father who testifies about Jesus (John 15:26).

The Holy Spirit illuminates believing women's hearts and minds. Today's followers of Christ will never have to stand in their own strength as they reflect on the great mystery and tragedy of God dying on a cross.

God's Written Word

Christian women today have access to God's written Word. The women who followed Christ heard him speak and teach the words of God, but they did not have the completed canon of Scripture—the sixty-six books of the Old and New Testaments.

Today women who follow Christ not only hide God's Word in their hearts but also hold it in their hands! We have written accounts of Christ's words and what transpired that fateful day, including these women's faithful testimony. And, because the Gospel writers carefully recorded the details of Christ's life and ministry, we can stand at the scene of the crucifixion and observe with both hindsight and insight!

For example, the truth the apostle John recorded in John 13:1 comforts us and brings the expression of God's love to this cruel scene. "Jesus knew that the time had come for him to leave this world and go to the Father. Having loved his own who were in the world, he now showed them the full extent of his love."

We read of Jesus's desire that Christians have the full measure of his joy within. Christ knew this would only be possible when he left and the Holy Spirit came to reside within his followers. Shortly before his arrest, Jesus prayed to the Father, "I am coming to you now, but I say these things while I am still in the world, so that they may have the full measure of my joy within them" (John 17:13).

Because of the Scriptures, today's Christian woman can see beyond the agony of Jesus's suffering to the victory—the very reason he came to that hour! She can marvel in the amazing simplicity of his words the day before he died: "I came from the Father and entered the world; now I am leaving the world and going back to the Father" (John 16:28).

Even though Christ spoke repeatedly about his imminent death, his words now reverberate with deep significance. "Do you think I cannot call on my Father, and he will at once put at my disposal more than twelve legions of angels? But how then would the Scriptures be fulfilled that say it must happen this way?" (Matt. 26:53).

The women followers of Christ listened as rabbis read from the Torah—the books of the Law and the Prophets. Christian women today possess their own personal copies of God's Word.

Christian women today no longer depend on others to read the Holy Scriptures to them—they can read them for themselves. Furthermore, they can select from a wide variety of translations and study formats, including recordings of the Bible. Reading, owning, and studying the completed Word of God makes today's Christian women the most privileged in the history of the church.

We Have an Example

In a powerful way, the lives and loyalties of the women at the cross provide models for women today. Their presence at the crucifixion allows other women to join with them in spirit. Their courage and faithfulness challenge us to stand with them and observe the love displayed on the cross.

Faithful women today join with Christian women throughout the history of the church in experiencing with fresh awareness Christ's great acts of love—becoming sin that we might know freedom from sin, experiencing death that we might escape spiritual death, and knowing God's rejection that we might know God's full acceptance.

Mary Magdalene, Mary the mother of Jesus, Mary's sister, Mary the wife of Clopas, Susanna, and Joanna never knew we would read and write about their commitment two thousand years later. We've learned that one generation models and mentors the next—a privilege but also a weighty responsibility.

Freedom to Celebrate

Christian women who choose to stand at the cross of Jesus Christ experience an amazing emotion—a spirit of celebration!

They have freedom to move past the agony of Jesus's suffering and see his victory, his goal, the very reason he came to that hour!

We not only read his words but also rejoice in them! Even though we experience sorrow knowing our Lord suffered for us, we also have cause for celebration—his joy, love, and peace can fill our hearts now and throughout eternity!

14

Remembering the Cross

And he took bread, gave thanks and broke it, and
gave it to them, saying, "This is my body given for
you; do this in remembrance of me."

Luke 22:19

The women at the cross never forgot what they saw at Golgotha. In Christ's foreknowledge, he provided ways for us to remember his sacrifice today. He brings our minds back to the work of the cross through the arts, Scripture, and prayer. We too can come face-to-face with God on the cross.

Through the Lord's Supper

During the last meal Christ shared with his disciples, he used bread and wine as symbols for his upcoming crucifixion. Then he told his followers to share the bread and wine as a way to remember.

> While they were eating, Jesus took bread, gave thanks and broke it, and gave it to his disciples saying, "Take and eat; this is my body." Then he took the cup, gave thanks and offered it to them, saying, "Drink from it, all of you. This is my blood of the covenant, which is poured out for many for the forgiveness of sins. I tell you, I will not drink of this fruit of the vine from now on until that day when I drink it anew with you in my Father's kingdom."
>
> Matthew 26:26–29

> Do this in remembrance of me.
>
> Luke 22:19

The early church used the phrase "breaking bread." Today we use different words to describe the memorial service—the Lord's Supper, the Eucharist, or communion. No matter what words we use, the ordinance impacts our lives. John Walvoord lists three perspectives it offers believers. "First, it looks to the past, reminding Christians of the Lord's redemptive sacrifice on the cross. Second, it looks to the present and the Christians' continuing fellowship with Christ as their Advocate and great high priest. Third, it looks to the future in anticipation of the imminent return of Christ."[1] Through the ordinance of the Lord's Supper, we too can stand before the Savior at Golgotha and observe that great demonstration of love.

Anne Dutton, a Calvinistic theological author of the eighteenth century, anonymously published a devotional study in 1748. She titled it "The Lord's Table, Thoughts on the Lord's Supper, Relating to the Nature, Subjects, and Right Partaking of this Solemn Ordinance." Anne viewed the Lord's Supper as a "royal banquet which infinite love hath prepared." In fact, she considered it "the nearest approach to his glorious Self that we can make in an ordinance . . . on this side [of] . . . his glory in heaven."[2]

In Anne's extravagant language of the mid-eighteenth century, she declared, "O what a wondrous draught, what a life-giving draught, in his own most precious blood, doth God our Savior, the Lord our Lover, give to dying sinners, to his beloved ones in this glorious ordinance."[3] Believers today might come together to share in the Lord's Supper with less formality than Anne Dutton's eighteenth-century experience, but we must never sacrifice sincerity. Paul admonishes us to examine ourselves—to search our hearts before God and acknowledge any sin that needs forgiveness (1 Cor. 11:29–32). As we receive pardon and cleansing, we have an opportunity to experience with the women before the cross a renewed devotion—as we observe once more God's great demonstration of love.

Through Art

Art forms such as music, drama, art, and dance serve as effective ways of bringing us to the crucifixion. Music, from contemporary to traditional hymns, reminds those who sing or hum along of the day Christ died for the sins of the world. Solitary guitars, bongo drums, children's voices, tribal chants, orchestras, choirs, CDs, radios, and satellite transmissions send forth the message in rhythm and song of God's great love demonstrated through his Son—reminding those who listen of his sacrifice.

When women watch a dramatization of Christ's death or stand before a gripping painting or marble sculpture, they remember. Whether they travel to see Michelangelo's famous *La Pieta* in Saint Peter's Basilica or view it in a picture book, the result remains the same—remembering. Magnificent stained-glass windows or discount store pictures on a shanty wall, a child's drawing or a sand sculpture on the beach have the same effect. Our minds return to an event that occurred more than two thousand years ago, and our hearts stir with his love.

The increased popularity of the cross as personal jewelry as well as home decor attests to its timelessness.

Movies also provide a gripping way to revisit the cross. From the silent movie version of *Ben Hur* and the classic *The Greatest Story Ever Told* to recent movies such as *The Gospel of John* and *The Passion*, the story draws us back to remember.

Through the Spoken and Written Word

The spoken word creates vivid pictures in the listener's mind of Christ's death. From local pulpits, television broadcasts, and small group Bible studies, the Good News of Christ's redemptive work on the cross draws listeners back to the crucifixion. Christ spoke his messages of love and salvation in Aramaic, but today almost fifteen hundred identified languages and dialects around the world communicate this eternal story.[4]

In addition to the spoken word, the message of Christ's blood is woven throughout all of Scripture. In Genesis, the first book of the Bible, we see the initial glimpse of a divine Redeemer who will deal a death blow to Satan's head through his death on the cross (Gen. 3:15–16).[5]

In the book of Revelation, John describes his vision of heaven and the presence of Jesus Christ as the sacrificial Lamb of God. "I did not see a temple in the city, because the Lord God Almighty and the Lamb are its temple. The city does not need the sun or the moon to shine on it, for the glory of God gives it light, and the Lamb is its light" (Rev. 21:22–23).

At the crucifixion, we witnessed an example of both the spoken word and the written Word. From the cross, Christ quoted the first verse of Psalm 22 when he cried out, "My God, my God, why have you forsaken me?" (Ps. 22:1). The remainder of the psalm graphically describes the Messiah's future death—long before the Roman Empire invented death by crucifixion.

> My God, my God, why have you forsaken me?
> > Why are you so far from saving me,
> > so far from the words of my groaning?
> O my God, I cry out by day, but you do not answer,
> > by night, and am not silent.
>
> But I am a worm and not a man,
> > scorned by men and despised by the people.
> All who see me mock me;
> > they hurl insults, shaking their heads:
> "He trusts in the LORD;
> > let the LORD rescue him.
> Let him deliver him,

since he delights in him."

Do not be far from me,
for trouble is near.
and there is no one to help.

I am poured out like water,
and all my bones are out of joint.
My heart has turned to wax;
it has melted away within me.
My strength is dried up like a potsherd,
and my tongue sticks to the roof of my mouth;
you lay me in the dust of death.
Dogs have surrounded me;
a band of evil men has encircled me,
they have pierced my hands and my feet.
I can count all my bones;
people stare and gloat over me.
They divide my garments among them
and cast lots for my clothing.

Psalm 22:1–2, 6–8, 11, 14–18

All of Scripture, from the first book, Genesis, through the last, Revelation, causes us to remember.

Through Worship and Prayer

Believers enter into God's presence in worship and prayer because of what Christ accomplished at Calvary. Those very acts acknowledge God's grace at the cross. Jesus spoke earlier of true worship to the Samaritan woman. He explained, "God is spirit, and his worshipers must worship in spirit and in truth" (John 4:24). Jesus knew that the entire structure of worship would soon change. Jerusalem had been the center of life and worship for the Jews. But because of the Lord's death, resurrection, and ascension, the place of worship is no longer important.

In addition to the freedom to worship in spirit, believers no longer offer animal sacrifices for sins or need earthly priests to intercede.[6] Christ became the great High Priest in heaven who intercedes for us, and he dispenses grace from his throne to everyone who comes to him in faith (Heb. 4:14–16). Hebrews 7:27 says, "Unlike the other high priests, he does not need to offer sacrifices day after day, first for his own sins, and then for the sins of the people. He sacrificed for their sins once for all when he offered himself."

We now worship through the power of the Holy Spirit and through the truth of who Christ is and what he accomplished. Our words of worship and prayer ascend to the very throne of God where Christ intercedes for us. Through the Lord's Supper, religious art, God's Word, worship, and prayer we remember Calvary and marvel at the wonder of God's grace.

15

Responding with Love and Faithfulness

Be imitators of God, therefore, as dearly loved
children and live a life of love, just as Christ loved
us and gave himself up for us as a fragrant offering
and sacrifice to God.

Ephesians 5:1

Even though we find female followers of Christ throughout the history of the church, we see something profound
in this gathering of women at the cross. As we view their
actions on Passover Friday, we observe an amazing level of
courage and devotion. We feel challenged to discover that

same passionate relationship with Christ and to follow him with devotion and service.

Love Christ Passionately

As we reflect on other women Christ directly influenced during his earthly ministry, such as the woman with the issue of blood, the woman at the well, and the woman caught in adultery (Mark 5:25–34; John 4:7; 8:4), we realize that a personal encounter with Jesus profoundly impacted each one. Have you discovered the loving, healing, merciful touch of Christ in your life?

The same relationship Mary Magdalene, Salome, Joanna, and the others had with the Son of God is available to women today. When their lives intersected with Christ, they each chose to respond to his forgiveness and healing touch. Have you also chosen to respond?[1]

Face Your Fears

Fear immobilizes and neutralizes followers of Christ. Does fear keep you from full commitment to Christ? Do you fear others' response? Perhaps you fear failure, afraid you'll turn back when things get too hard or too stressful. Does fear of hardships prevent you from following Christ to difficult areas of the world? Would identifying yourself publicly as a friend of Christ jeopardize job advancement, family relationships, or even your life?

Linda Petty, widowed at age forty-seven, realized this season of her life provided opportunities to serve Christ. Her heart's passion, loving children who had no one to love them, prompted her to sell her husband's business and relocate to Nigeria. Linda worked with Rafiki Foundation[2] to establish an orphanage for children whose parents had died from AIDS. In the past three years, she has escaped from a raging house fire, faced homesickness, and coped with frustratingly slow progress. She has also discovered the delight of smiling babies, a strengthened faith, and the deep abiding joy of faithfully serving her Lord.

From the earliest believers who pressed through their personal fears at the cross, women have chosen faith over fear. Their courage prompts us to find our own strength in Christ and to remain faithful even in our fear.

Move Out from the Crowd

Some believers prefer the safety and anonymity of a group. Does the thought of stepping out of obscurity to lead spark feelings of inadequacy? Does a lack of confidence hide behind a wall of excuses?

The women who moved from the distant crowd to stand closer to Jesus on the cross responded to an opportunity. The soldiers allowed the mother of Jesus and the others to quietly approach the cross for final parting words. They looked directly upward at the face of Christ. In his eyes they saw love in the midst of agony and compassion in response to brutality.

Until recently, Kalena Crews preferred the safety of the crowd. Even though she excelled professionally as a registered nurse, she hesitated to step out into leadership among her peers. Today she teaches a singles' Sunday morning Bible study group. It took courage to step forward, but she followed the prompting of her heart and discovered the rewarding challenge of moving beyond the crowd.

We frequently have opportunities to step forward to speak a word of comfort, to offer a soothing touch, or to express Christ's presence. When we respond, we always receive more than we give. Not only do we sense Christ's loving gaze of approval, but we also go away changed by the experience.

Be Effective in Your Spheres of Influence

The women in attendance at Golgotha represented diverse life experiences. They included:

- women with financial resources and women of modest means
- women with political and social influence and women from obscurity
- women who knew mental illness, spiritual illness, or physical illness
- women from metropolitan areas and women from small villages
- women with formal education and women with no education
- women called to godly parenting and women without children
- women with husbands, widowed women, and single women

Each woman, regardless of her situation, used her experiences and resources in serving Christ. Christian women today also represent diverse lifestyles. A painful divorce thrust Donna Shay into the struggling world of working single moms. Donna now serves Christ in the arena of real estate, using her unique opportunities to influence others for Christ. She ranks as one of her company's top salespersons. Demonstrating Christ's love to her clients remains, though, her number one passion. She not only commits to helping clients locate the right house, she also makes herself available to help others locate a Savior and a church home where they can grow in their faith.

Remain Faithful to Your Task

The women who served Christ during his earthly ministry brought their life experiences, their resources, and themselves to Christ's ministry. The inconvenience of life on the road, the hostile religious leaders, and daily tasks of serving failed to deter them.

Anne Murchison discovered the healing power of God's love as an adult while living with her fourth husband, Clint Murchison. For eighteen months, a Christian friend came weekly to disciple Anne and to teach her God's Word—setting her on the path to a transformed life.[3] Today Anne faithfully mentors other women and teaches them God's Word. Through her husband's terminal illness, the bankruptcy of his multimillion-dollar estate, the death of her mentally ill mother, and her son's diagnosis of schizophrenia, Anne remained faithful in her service to the God she loved. She learned to remain faithful even when the day grew dark and the earth quaked beneath her feet.

Be a Good Steward

Jewish women of the first century rarely had control of much money, yet Scripture records that they supported Christ out of their own finances. Since the Gospels do not identify the source of their income, we can only guess. Perhaps they crafted items for the market or sold produce from their gardens.

Few women had a family inheritance as a source of money, because the inheritance went to the firstborn son. A woman's husband managed what she received from her father in the marriage contract—or "ketubbah." The resources returned to her only if her husband died.[4]

Whatever the source of the money, these women had a heart to give it. God had chosen and prepared them especially to fill this role. They offered themselves as conduits of God's blessings and provision for his Son. God does the same today! God chooses women for similar purposes—to facilitate the flow of financial resources in his work around the world.

Gay Brookshire serves on the board of Royal Treasure, a nonprofit organization focused on educating women on the stewardship of giving. Gay not only desires to grow in her personal financial stewardship, but encourages other women to join with her. Together they seek God's guidance in intentional giving. They also seek to grow in their knowledge of how to appropriately manage their resources for God's kingdom. Gay joins with the women at the cross as well as those through the ages in her faithful stewardship of God's gifts.

Learn from Christ

Jesus went against the customs of his culture in allowing women to learn from him. Women in many countries today continue to break cultural constraints as they personally study and teach God's Word—sometimes under threat of imprisonment or death.

Miss B. remembers learning simple Bible stories at her mother's feet as a small child in China during Mao Tse-tung's Cultural Revolution.[5] After her father's brutal beating because of his Christian faith, the regime sent the family to an isolated area of Tibet for the duration of Mao's rule.

During those years, Miss B. continued to learn through her mother's handwritten copy of the Bible hidden behind the cover of Mao's government issued *Little Red Book*. Today Miss B. continues to passionately study and teach God's Word—in spite of numerous prison sentences and personal suffering.

Unprecedented numbers of women around the world now have the opportunity to participate in personal Bible study groups. In countries with religious freedom, Christian bookstores offer shelves of Bible studies and books written by women for women. In addition, a growing number of women of all ages choose to leave the comforts of home to bring God's Word to those who have never heard.

Offer Yourself to Others as to Christ

God equipped women with the ability to demonstrate God's love and emotional presence to others. God values the simple acts of holding a hand, writing a note, making a phone

125

call, or offering a hug. Sitting silently or quietly listening demonstrates God's own tenderness and concern.

Sue Herron sensitively and faithfully demonstrates God's concern through sending cards or writing letters. Sometimes she sends them purposefully in response to special events like birthdays or anniversaries. At other times, she sends them in response to the prompting of the Holy Spirit. Over the years, Sue's encouraging words through notes have delivered God's strength right to the front doors of friends, acquaintances, and missionaries around the world. Sue demonstrates how women followers of Christ can use loving actions, no matter how small, to express their own love for God.

Learn How Both to Serve and Sit

Some of the women at the cross knew the frustration of juggling roles. They knew the demands of maintaining both a home and a relationship with a husband. Some coped with expectations of their children. Yet even with these distractions, they learned to take their cues from Jesus. Sometimes they busily "tended" to things—shopping, meal preparation, and laundry. At other times, they joined with the disciples or the crowds to absorb Christ's teachings or to wonder at his miracles.

Marsha Lester and Betty Wall have discovered that same balance in their lives. Monday afternoons they arrive at their church to set up attractive refreshment tables for the following morning's Bible studies. The aroma of freshly brewed coffee and fresh pastries says "welcome" to the women arriving the next morning. Marsha and Betty also actively participate in the ongoing Bible study groups. Then, after everyone has departed, they remain to clean up—all the while with cheerful smiles! They have learned to balance serving their Lord and learning from him.

These women followers of Christ challenge us to rise to new levels of faithfulness. Their lives mentor us. The expression of our own faith rises to new levels as a result of observing the women at the cross. May our faithfulness as followers of Christ also be a source of inspiration and encouragement for today's generation and the ones yet to come.

16

Living at the Foot of the Cross

We know and rely on the love God has for us.

1 John 4:16

God continues to seek out women whose lives form a vital link in this ongoing lineage of faithful women—just as he did with our earliest Christian sisters and those throughout church history. Herbert Lockyer, in the introduction to his extensive book *All the Women of the Bible*, writes that in his study of women of the Bible, he discovered an impressive fact: "the . . . women in Bible times find an echo in the traits of women today."[1] God extends the invitation to *all* women.

To those women drawn to the cross today, I'd like to offer four suggestions: know your value to Christ, feel his loving embrace in your life, experience the joy of joining in God's great work, and worship at the cross as you live out your life.

Know Your Value to Christ

Christ valued the unique qualities women brought to his ministry—devotion, loyalty, and a servant's heart. Jesus also ignored the Middle Eastern culture that prevented men from speaking to women in public.[2] Jesus not only spoke with them publicly, but also incorporated them into his ministry—and he still does! Christ continues to include women from cultures all over the world as integral parts of his kingdom's work.

One of the great preachers of our day, W. A. Criswell, noticed in his studies that "Jesus never used a woman as an illustration for evil, never asked a woman one incriminating question, and never caused a woman to experience shame."[3] This amazing observation prompts us to marvel and ask the question, "Why?" Christ spoke directly and sometimes sharply when talking to men. Why would Jesus use such restraint when speaking to women?

On occasions deserving of reprimand, Christ spoke to women directly—but without an attitude of condemnation. Christ treated women the way God designed them to be treated. Christ, who knows all things, knows women. The Creator of women spoke to his creation in their heart language—in a way that gave them the freedom to respond from deep within.

Instead of deriving your value from the world's view of women, from friends, work, men, magazines, or the mirror— look to Christ! Immerse yourself in his words. Ask his Spirit to transform your mind and heart into his very own. Live your life forgiven and whole, viewing his love from the foot of the cross.

Feel God's Loving Embrace

God desires that women everywhere feel the embrace of the unconditional love, acceptance, and affirmation Jesus offers. I pray that you might move beyond your hesitations of how you *expect* Jesus to respond and approach him with emotional abandon.

Christ's words to the woman caught in adultery set her free: "Woman, where are they? Has no one condemned you? . . . Go now and leave your life of sin" (John 8:10–11). To the Samaritan woman at the well, Christ offered the gift of living water—"a spring of water welling up to eternal life" (John 4:14).

Open your heart to Christ's embrace. Trust him completely to bring you to repentance, not shame, and to a life of rewarding devotion, not bondage. When women everywhere begin to feel Christ's tender embrace, their lives will demonstrate, in response, passionate commitment—*and the world will be changed by it!*

Join in Christ's Great Work

After Christ's ascension, Luke recorded that the disciples "joined together constantly in prayer, along with the women and Mary the mother of Jesus" (Acts 1:14). Together they waited for the empowerment of the Holy Spirit. As momentum builds toward the return of Christ, I pray that you will actively join with the body of Christ empowered by the Holy Spirit. Experience the impact that results when believers work together to spread the unfathomable message of salvation accomplished that great day at Calvary.

Worship at the Cross

Last, may we live our lives approaching the cross of Christ with the wonder, devotion, and thanksgiving worthy of our Savior's love. When struggling with sinful desires, return to the cross and claim Christ's victory over the power of sin. When feelings of rejection, abandonment, or shame encroach, remember Christ's experiences on Calvary. As you seek to forgive, ask Christ to forgive through you just as he forgave the soldiers who hung him on the cross. When struggling with accepting God's will for your life, call upon that same submissiveness Christ demonstrated to his Father's will. And during dark days when fear of death or death of a loved one encroaches, remember that Christ conquered death and lives forever.

Isaac Watts used a feather quill and an inkwell over two hundred years ago to capture his own devotion as he worshiped Christ. He distilled the source of a faithful follower's devotion to one short phrase—"Love so amazing, so divine, demands my soul, my life, my *all*."[4]

Appendix

Putting It All Together

Christians experience many blessings of salvation, like prayer, in a day-to-day practical way. Other blessings, like justification, profoundly affect our lives even though we seldom stop to consider them. The following summary statements offer a tool to help us better understand these vital foundations for the Christian life.

Atonement—restoration of a broken relationship

Atonement describes the restoration of the broken relationship between God and humankind. Through Christ's sacrifice that canceled our sins, he reinstates us to a relationship of at-one-ment with God. "He is the atoning sacrifice for our sins, and not only for ours but also for the sins of the whole world" (1 John 2:2).

Reconciliation—being brought back into relationship

Reconciliation describes the process by which God brings people back into a relationship with him. It involves a changed relationship because our trespasses no longer count against us. Reconciliation affects both God and the believer. Christ's sacrifice atoned for people's sins and also appeased God's wrath and judgment of sin. "For if, when we were God's enemies, we were reconciled to him through the death of his Son, how much more, having been reconciled, shall we be saved through his life! Not only is this so, but we also rejoice in God through our Lord Jesus Christ, through whom we have now received reconciliation" (Rom. 5:10–11).

Redemption—the act of buying back

Redemption describes the process by which God judicially declares believing sinners righteous and acceptable before God. Christ paid the ransom our sin demanded. As a result, we are set free from the bondage of sin and made righteous and acceptable before him. "In him we have redemption through his blood, the forgiveness of sins, in accordance with the riches of God's grace that he lavished on us with all wisdom and understanding" (Eph. 1:7–8).

Justification—making someone acceptable to God

Justification describes the process by which Jesus made sinful human beings acceptable to a holy God, just as if they had never sinned. The infinite holy judge judicially declares righteous those who believe in Jesus (Rom. 8:31–34). When God justifies, he charges the sin of man to Christ and credits the righteousness of Christ to the believer. "He was delivered over to death for our sins and was raised to life for our justification. . . .

The result of one act of righteousness was justification that brings life for all men" (Rom. 4:25; 5:18).

Sanctification—the process of growing in Christ

Sanctification describes the process by which believers grow to maturity in Christ. The Word of God and the Holy Spirit produce holiness—purification from the guilt and power of sin. God's grace separates the believers from sin and sets them apart for God's righteousness and service. "For them I sanctify myself, that they too may be truly sanctified" (John 17:19).

Because Christ died on the cross:

His *atonement* (the sacrifice that cancels my sin)
brings me into *reconciliation* (a restored relationship with God)
through the process of *redemption* (setting me free).
As a result, my *justification* (being declared not guilty)
leads to a life of *sanctification* (growing in maturity in Christ).

God wants you to know these blessings for yourself—just like the women who followed Jesus before you. Seek God in faith with your whole heart. Prayer offers a way to express your faith in Christ and your belief that he died for your sins. Prayer simply uses words, silently or audibly, to express your heart to God. Here's an example: *Dear Jesus, I admit that I am a sinner. I believe you died on the cross for my sins. Please forgive my sins, and fill my life with your love and your Holy Spirit. Amen.*

Take time to pray right now, then let someone know! They'll want to rejoice with you!

Notes

Introduction

1. Oswald Chambers, *My Utmost for His Highest* (Westwood, NJ: Barbour, 1935), 330–31.

Chapter 1: The Crucifixion Scene

1. Because the original Greek language used no punctuation marks, some believe the phrase "Mary the wife of Clopas" refers to the sister of Mary the mother of Jesus. Others believe these were two different women.

2. "Normally a person in the last stages of crucifixion would not have the strength to speak beyond a weak groan, but each synoptic Gospel says that Jesus spoke with a 'loud voice.' Jesus's words came from Psalm 31:5, which Jews used as an evening prayer. To the Christian reader who knows that Jesus's death was a voluntary act, they are beautifully appropriate. All four Gospels describe Jesus's moment of death in terse, restrained words" (Frank E. Gaebelein, *The Expositor's Bible Commentary* [Grand Rapids: Zondervan, 1984], 1045).

Chapter 2: The Women and Their World

1. Joachim Jeremias, *Jerusalem in the Time of Jesus* (Philadelphia: Fortress, 1969), 375.

2. Ibid., a prayer recommended for daily use.

3. Ibid., 369.

4. Ibid., 373.

5. Ibid.

6. Tal Ilan, *Jewish Women in Greco-Roman Palestine* (Peabody, MA: Hendrickson, 1996), 54.

7. Mark 15:40; Luke 8:3; 24:10; *The Woman's Study Bible*, ed. Dorothy Kelley Patterson (Nashville: Thomas Nelson, 1995), 1680, 1707, 1746.

8. Gilbert V. Beers, *The Victor Journey through the Bible* (Colorado Springs: Cook, 1981), 286.

9. Galileans had a reputation for being pious and passionate. Both of these qualities were necessary for these women to break tradition and face scandal as they left their homes to travel with a rabbi.

10. In Luke 23:49 the word "accompanied" is a translation of the Greek word *sunakoloutheo*, which very likely speaks of discipleship, yet it does not capture the full significance of their role in this context. See Boyd Luter and Kathy McReynolds, *Women as Christ's Disciples* (Grand Rapids: Baker, 1997), 26.

Chapter 3: The Women from Galilee

1. Ruth A. Tucker and Walter Liefeld, *Daughters of the Church: Women and Ministry from New Testament Times to the Present* (Grand Rapids: Zondervan, 1987), 23.

2. Ibid.

3. "Josephus said Magdala had 4,000 inhabitants and 230 boats. The Talmud tells us it had 80 weavers' shops and 300 shops that sold pigeons for sacrifices. . . ." The city's horse and chariot race track indicates it also had a large Gentile population worshiping pagan gods. This might have been a strong influence on Mary's demon possession. See Beers, *Victor Journey*, 335.

4. The only exception is John 19:25, where there is a special interest in Jesus's mother. See "Mary Magdalene," in Luter and McReynolds, *Women*, 70.

5. "Greco-Roman society as a whole was highly superstitious with belief in magic widespread, even among the Jews. These practices naturally left the door open to the demonic world. It could be that Mary Magdalene either participated in or was influenced by these beliefs. The fact that seven demons were cast out of her indicates that she must have been actively involved with the powers of darkness to some degree" (Luter and McReynolds, *Women*, 68).

6. Merrill F. Unger, *The New Unger's Bible Dictionary*, rev. ed., ed. R. K. Harrison (Chicago: Moody, 1988), 1379.

7. Beers, *Victor Journey*, 326. Herod Antipas's original capital was in Sepphoris, only four miles from Nazareth, until he relocated the capital in AD 25 to Tiberias.

8. "By comparing John 19:25 with Luke 24:18 and Matthew 10:3, it appears that Alphaeus is the Greek and Cleopas or Clopas, the Hebrew . . . name of the same person" (Unger, *Bible Dictionary*, 243).

9. "Many modern critics are of the opinion that Salome was the sister of Mary, the mother of Jesus, alluded to in John 19:25. Others make the expression 'His

mother's sister' refer to 'Mary the wife of Clopas,' immediately following" (Unger, *Bible Dictionary*, 1113).

Chapter 4: Passions at the Cross of Christ

1. Barry Hudson, "The Women at the Cross," Trenton Church of Christ Bulletin, July 2, 2000. Reading Room, www.svic.net/kerux/b2juloo.htm.

Chapter 5: The Women's Offering

1. The Greek word *ochloi* refers to a mixed group of people, "all the people" (*Expositor's Bible Commentary*, 8:1046).

2. Luter and McReynolds, *Women*, 72.

3. Ibid., 23.

4. *Kenosis*; lit., "emptying"; i.e., What were the limitations of the incarnate Christ on earth? (Charles Ryrie, *Ryrie Study Bible*, "The Doctrine of Christ: The Kenosis," Philippians 2:7, 1760).

5. S. E. Taylor, L. C. Klein, B. P. Lewis, T. L. Gruenewald, R. A. R. Gurung, and J. A. Updegraff, "Female Responses to Stress: Tend and Befriend, Not Fight or Flight," *Psychological Review* 107, no. 3 (2000): 41, as cited in Gale Berkowitz, "UCLA Study on Friendship Among Women," http://www.psc.uc.edu/news/stressfriendship women.htm.

Chapter 6: The Burial

1. Exodus 35:3. *New Unger's Bible Dictionary*, s.v. "Sabbath."

2. John 19:31–34. *Wycliff Bible Commentary*, New Testament, edited by Charles F. Pfeiffer and Everett F. Harrison (Chicago: Moody, 1962), 314.

3. H. L. Willmington, *Willmington's Guide to the Bible* (Wheaton: Tyndale House, 1982), 314, 335.

Chapter 7: The Visit to the Tomb

1. "Angels appear and disappear at pleasure, according to the orders and instructions given them. . . . This favor was shown to those who were early and constant in their inquiries after Christ and was the reward of those who came first and stayed last" (*Bethany Parallel Commentary on the New Testament* [Minneapolis: Bethany, 1983], 682).

2. Also an idle tale (*leros*). *Leros* is a strong term used only here in the New Testament. It refers to nonsense or empty talk, "pure nonsense" (Darrell L. Bock, ed., *The Bible Knowledge Key Word Study, the Gospels* [Colorado Springs: Victor, 2002], 256).

3. *Rabboni* means "teacher."

4. Adam Clarke, in *Bethany Parallel Commentary*, 682.

5. Luter and McReynolds, *Women*, 24.

6. Gilbert Bilezikian, *Beyond Sex Roles* (Grand Rapids: Baker, 1985), 104, quoted in Tucker and Liefeld, *Daughters*, 39.

7. Luter and McReynolds, *Women*, 28.

Chapter 8: Sharing the Good News

1. Lawrence O. Richards, *New Testament Life and Times* (Colorado Springs: Cook, 1994), 46.

2. K. Schilder, *Christ in His Suffering*, trans. H. Zylstra (Grand Rapids: Eerdmans, 1938), 289–309. *Expositor's Bible Commentary*, 8:543.

3. Ibid., 560.

4. *Nelson's New Illustrated Bible Dictionary*, ed. Ronald F. Youngblood (Nashville: Thomas Nelson, 1995), 420.

5. Chambers, *My Utmost for His Highest*, 325.

Chapter 9: Women Who Served through Suffering

1. Edith Deen, *Great Women of the Christian Faith* (New York: Harper & Row, 1959), 4.

2. Ibid.

3. See "The Passion of the Holy Martyrs Perpetua and Felicitas" at http://bible1.crosswalk.com/History/AD/EarlyChurchFathers/Ante-Nicene/Tertullian/view.cgi?file=anf03-54.htm&word=perpetua&size=20.

4. Ibid.

5. Ibid.

6. Routh, *Reliquiae*, as cited in "The Passion of the Holy Martyrs," 358.

7. Ibid.

8. Ibid.

9. John D. Woodbridge, ed., *Great Leaders of the Christian Church* (Chicago: Moody, 1988), 178.

10. *The Dialogue* or *Treatise on Divine Providence* ranks among the classics of the Italian language. It can be found at www.newadvent.org.

11. Gospelcom.net, Glimpses Issue #46, "Ann Hasseltine Judson: First American Woman Missionary," http://www.gospelcom.net/chi/GLIMPSEF/Glimpses/glmps046.shtml.

12. Ibid.

13. Ibid.

14. *American Baptist Magazine* 4 (January 1923): 20, quoted in Tucker and Liefeld, *Daughters*, 296.

Chapter 10: Women Who Opened Their Homes

1. *The Complete Who's Who in the Bible*, ed. Paul D. Gardner (Grand Rapids: Zondervan, 1995), 551.

2. William Barclay, *The Letter to the Romans* (Philadelphia: Westminster, 1955), 52.

3. Eugenia Price, *God Speaks to Women Today* (Grand Rapids: Zondervan, 1964), 238.

4. Barclay, *Letter to the Romans*, 210.

5. A translation known as the Vulgate, the official translation of the Roman church for the next one thousand years.

6. *Eerdmans' Handbook to the History of Christianity*, ed. Tim Dowley (Grand Rapids: Eerdmans, 1977), 360–66.

7. Deen, *Great Women*, 90.

8. Gospelcom.net, "Katie von Bora Sets the Tone for Lutheran Wives," http://www.gospelcom.net/chi/women/bora.shtml.

9. Ibid.

10. Gospelcom.net, Glimpses Issue #154, "Highlights of Luther's Life in His Own Words," http://www.gospelcom.net/chi/GLIMPSEF/Glimpses/glmps154.shtml.

11. Ibid.

12. Tucker and Liefeld, *Daughters*, 237.

13. Gospelcom.net, Glimpses Issue #77, "O Susanna: Model of a Christian Mother," http://www.gospelcom.net/chi/GLIMPSEF/Glimpses/glmps077.shtml.

14. Ibid.

15. *Eerdmans' Handbook*, 447–49.

Chapter 11: Women Who Influenced through Their Resources

1. Deen, *Great Women*, 29.

2. Ibid., 32.

3. Ibid., 74.

4. Ibid., 76. "These compositions were almost all inspired by conversations he had with Vittoria Colonna" (Valerio Mariani, *Michelangelo* [New York: Abrams, 1966], 140).

5. Deen, *Great Women*, 76.

6. Ibid., 81.

7. Ibid., 182.

8. Ibid., 184.

9. Ibid., 185.

Chapter 12: Women Who Instructed and Encouraged

1. Bede (673–735), the most respected and talented historian of the early Middle Ages, spent almost his entire life in North England monasteries. His work is marked by careful attention to sources and facts as opposed to legend. Bede popularized the calendar using the birth of Christ as the baseline for events. *Eerdmans' Handbook*, 14.

2. Deen, *Great Women*, 37.

3. Ibid., 258. The friend was the Reverend J. Krehbiel. See also pp. 251–55.

4. Gospelcom.net, Remarkable Christian Women: "Pandita Ramabai and India's Downtrodden Women," http://www.gospelcom.net/chi/women/ramabai.shtml.

5. Deen, *Great Women*, 282.

Chapter 13: Women of the Twenty-first Century

1. Helen Hosier, *100 Christian Women Who Changed the 20th Century* (Grand Rapids: Revell, 2000).

Chapter 14: Remembering the Cross

1. Don Campbell, Wendell Johnston, John Walvoord, and John Witmer, *The Theological Wordbook* (Waco: Word, 2000), 229.

2. Anne Dutton, 1672–1765, "Previously Asked Questions # 1864004," www.allexperts.com.

3. Ibid.

4. "Individual dialects identify a 'people group.' To date, 1497 people groups representing five billion of the world's 6.5 billion people have access to the Gospel of Christ. An additional 5007 people groups, referred to as 'The Last Frontier,' represent one billion people who do not currently have access to the Gospel of Christ." International Mission Board of the Southern Baptist Convention, "Fast Facts" brochure, 2003.

5. "He," meaning "an individual from among the woman's seed, namely, Christ," would deal a death blow to Satan's "head" at the cross, while Satan ("*you*") would strike Christ's "heel" causing him to suffer. *Ryrie Study Bible* NIV, 11.

6. Campbell, et al., *Theological Wordbook*, 393.

Chapter 15: Responding with Love and Faithfulness

1. See the appendix, "Putting It All Together," for guidance in responding to Christ's love.

2. The Rafiki Foundation, Inc., 19001 Huebner Road #2, San Antonio, TX 78258-4040. Phone 210-244-2600.

3. Anne Ferrell Murchison, *Milk for Babes* (Waco: Word, 1979), 30.

4. "Inheritance," *Jewish Women*, 167.

5. Name changed to protect identity.

Chapter 16: Living at the Foot of the Cross

1. Herbert Lockyer, *All the Women of the Bible* (Grand Rapids: Zondervan, 1987), Introduction.

2. Men also were not allowed to speak in public to a wife, mother, or sister (see "The Samaritan Woman," *Woman's Study Bible*, 1758).

3. W. A. Criswell sermon notes, "She Hath Done What She Could," September 1991, http://www.wacriswell.org/index.cfm/FuseAction/Search.Outlines/Sermon/868.cfm.

4. Isaac Watts, "When I Survey the Wondrous Cross."

Bibliography

Barclay, William. *The Letter to the Romans*. Philadelphia: Westminster, 1955.

Beasley-Murray, George R. *John*. Vol. 36 of *Word Biblical Commentary*. Waco: Word, 1987.

Beers, Gilbert V. *The Victor Journey through the Bible*. Colorado Springs: Cook, 1981.

Bethany Parallel Commentary on the New Testament, The. Minneapolis: Bethany, 1983.

Bock, Darrell L., ed. *The Bible Knowledge Key Word Study. The Gospels*. Colorado Springs: Victor, 2002.

Campbell, Don, et al., *The Theological Wordbook: The 200 Most Important Theological Terms and Their Relevance for Today*. Waco: Word, 2000.

Chambers, Oswald. *My Utmost for His Highest*. Westwood, NJ: Barbour, 1935.

Deen, Edith. *All the Women of the Bible*. New York: Harper & Row, 1955.

———. *Great Women of the Christian Faith*. New York: Harper & Row, 1959.

Dowley, Tim, ed. *Eerdmans' Handbook to the History of Christianity*. Grand Rapids: Eerdmans, 1977.

Dunn, James D. G., and John Rogerson, eds. *Eerdmans' Commentary on the Bible*. Grand Rapids: Eerdmans, 2003.

Gaebelein, Frank E., ed. *The Expositor's Bible Commentary*. Vol. 8. Grand Rapids: Zondervan, 1984.

Gardner, Paul D., ed. *The Complete Who's Who in the Bible*. Grand Rapids: Zondervan, 1995.

George, Elizabeth. *Women Who Loved God*. Eugene: Harvest House, 1999.

Godwin, Johnnie C. *Layman's Bible Book, Mark*. Vol. 16. Nashville: Broadman, 1979.

Hebrew Greek Key Study Bible, New American Standard. Chattanooga, TN: AMG, 1984, 1999.

Hobbs, Herschel. *The Illustrated Life of Jesus*. Nashville: Holman, 2000.

Hosier, Helen Kooiman. *100 Christian Women Who Changed the 20th Century*. Grand Rapids: Revell, 2000.

Ilan, Tal. *Jewish Women in Greco-Roman Palestine*. Peabody, MA: Hendrickson, 1996.

Jeremias, Joachim. *Jerusalem in the Time of Jesus*. Philadelphia: Fortress, 1969.

Keener, Craig. *Bible Background Commentary, New Testament*. Downers Grove: InterVarsity Press, 1993.

Lockyer, Herbert. *All the Women of the Bible*. Grand Rapids: Zondervan, 1987.

Luter, Boyd, and Kathy McReynolds. *Women as Christ's Disciples*. Grand Rapids: Baker, 1997.

Lutz, Lorry. *Women as Risk-Takers for God*. Grand Rapids: Baker, 1997.

MacDonald, William. *Believer's Bible Commentary*. Nashville: Nelson, 1995.

Murchison, Anne Ferrell. *Milk for Babes*. Waco: Word, 1979.

Murphey, Cecil B., comp. *Dictionary of Biblical Literacy*. Nashville: Oliver-Nelson, 1989.

Osbeck, Kenneth W. "Lead Me to Calvary." In *Hallelujah, What a Savior!: 25 Hymn Stories Celebrating Christ Our Redeemer.* Grand Rapids: Kregel, 2000.

Patterson, Dorothy Kelley, ed. *The Woman's Study Bible.* Nashville: Nelson, 1995.

Pfeiffer, Charles F., and Everett F. Harrison, eds. *Wycliff Bible Commentary.* Chicago: Moody, 1962.

Price, Eugenia. *God Speaks to Women Today.* Grand Rapids: Zondervan, 1964.

Sproul, R.C., and Robert Wolgemuth. *What's in the Bible: The Story of God through Time and Eternity.* Nashville: Word, 2000.

Spurgeon, Charles H. *Spurgeon's Sermons on New Testament Women, Book One.* Grand Rapids: Kregel, 1994.

Stephens, Shirley. *A New Testament View of Women.* Nashville: Broadman, 1980.

Tertullian, "The Passion of the Holy Martyrs Perpetua and Felicitas." http://bible1.crosswalk.com/History/AD/EarlyChurchFathers/Ante-Nicene/Tertullian/view.cgi?file=anf03-54.htm&word=perpetua&size=20.

Tucker, Ruth A., and Walter Liefeld. *Daughters of the Church: Women and Ministry from New Testament Times to the Present.* Grand Rapids: Zondervan, 1987.

Unger, Merrill F. *The New Unger's Bible Dictionary.* Rev. ed. Edited by R. K. Harrison. Chicago: Moody, 1988.

Webster, Joann C., and Karen Davis, eds. *A Celebration of Women, Our Greatest Feats, Our Favorite Stories, Our Richest Legacy.* Southlake, TX: Watercolor Books, 2001.

Willmington, H. L. *Willmington's Guide to the Bible.* Wheaton: Tyndale, 1982.

Witherington, Ben. *Women in the Ministry of Jesus.* New York: Cambridge University Press, 1984.

Woodbridge, John D., ed. *Great Leaders of the Christian Church.* Chicago: Moody, 1988.

Youngblood, Ronald F., ed. *Nelson's New Illustrated Bible Dictionary.* Nashville: Nelson, 1995.

Discussion Questions

Chapter One

1. Read 2 Peter 1:19; Revelation 21:22–25; and 22:5, then discuss the symbolism of darkness and night in Scripture.
2. How do you think the women responded to the darkness during the crucifixion?
3. Read Matthew 27:54 and discuss the possible emotional impact of the earthquake on the women. Share a time when you felt extreme fear.
4. Roman law banned public displays of mourning at crucifixions. How do you think these restrictions affected the women at the cross as they coped with their grief?

Chapter Two

1. The women Jesus addressed as "daughters of Jerusalem" possibly followed Jesus as seekers of truth. Share a profile of a modern-day seeker and a time when you sought God.
2. Other women following Christ to Golgotha grieved for their "good teacher." How is reading God's Word similar or different from what the women heard as they listened to Jesus teach?
3. Read John 21:25 and imagine evening discussions as the women reviewed the day together.
4. How can women observe Christ's miracles and listen to his teaching today?

Chapter Three

1. Historians must search diligently for information on women during the time of Christ. Most names are limited to legal documents like marriage papers. Even tombstones often simply listed the word *wife* in place of the woman's name. How does God's recording the names of the women at the crucifixion increase the significance of their presence?
2. Brothers and sisters share unique bonding (positive or negative). Share a time a family member supported you in a crisis.
3. Read Ephesians 1:3–23 and ask God to increase awareness of your value to God.
4. Which verses in Ephesians 1:3–23 especially speak to your heart?

Verse 3;10 ᵉ this was His purpose to gather all (heaven & earth) to be with Him forever.

150

Chapter Four

1. Christ's followers had expectations of Jesus. Share a time when dashed expectations caused emotional pain.
2. How would you guide someone in placing expectations of her spouse, job, or children under Christ's sovereignty?
3. Simeon said, "A sword shall pierce your heart," in describing Mary's pain. Share a modern-day analogy for the pain of losing a child to death.
4. Nakedness (Jesus most likely wore no loincloth) plus loss of control of body functions due to dehydration and positioning of the body added to the shame of crucifixion. Hebrews 12:2 says Jesus scorned the shame, refusing to give it power over him. Identify shame in your life that you need to reject. Share only as you feel led and only at appropriate levels of disclosure.

Chapter Five

1. Recent research suggests women often respond to stress by seeking out other women. How do you think the women at the cross provided support for one another? Share a personal experience.
2. Read Psalm 86:15; Isaiah 40:11; 63:15; Matthew 23:37; and James 5:11, noting the qualities of God.
3. Women fear emotional abandonment. Read Hebrews 13:5–6 and John 17:24–26 to discover God's provision for that fear.
4. Share a time of emotional abandonment and how you found comfort from Christ.

Chapter Six

1. Joseph of Arimathea secretly followed Christ. Yet he openly revealed his allegiance on the day of Jesus's execution. Share a time when you lived as a secret follower of Christ.

2. Mary Magdalene and Mary the wife of Clopas created a tiny funeral procession when they followed Joseph and Nicodemus to the tomb. How do you think God viewed the presence of the women, Joseph, and Nicodemus?

3. Share a graveside experience when friends and family provided comfort.

4. Read Jesus's response to a friend's death in John 11:33–36. He conquered the "sting" or permanency of death a few days later. How does that victory affect your feelings toward death?

Chapter Seven

1. Read Christ's first recorded words after his resurrection in John 20:15. What does this question reveal about Christ?

2. Read about cherubim on the ark of the covenant in Exodus 37:7–8. What symbolism do you see in the angels at the head and the foot of where Christ had been laid?

3. God uses symbolism in nature to portray spiritual truths. Share a time when you saw God's handiwork and reflected upon a biblical truth.

4. God accomplished victory over death while the women waited throughout the Sabbath and the night that followed. When they arrived at the tomb, Jesus rewarded

their waiting with a personal visit. When have you struggled with "waiting on God"?

Chapter Eight

1. Read 1 Corinthians 2:10–13. Where would you place your personal spiritual maturity using a scale of infant, adolescent, young adult, adult, or senior adult?
2. What are your plans for future growth?
3. Turn to the appendix and read definitions of atonement, reconciliation, redemption, justification, and sanctification. Share your response to the following summary: "Because Christ died on the cross, his *atonement* brings me into *reconciliation* through the process of *redemption*. As a result, my *justification* leads to a life of *sanctification*."
4. Read Romans 8:13 and give a personal example of victory over sin through the power of the Spirit.

Chapter Nine

1. Read Psalm 116:5 and discuss how Perpetua brought glory to Christ through her refusal to deny him as Savior.
2. The phrase, "She is clothed in strength and dignity," describes the Proverbs 31 woman. In what ways did Ann Judson, Catherine of Siena, and Perpetua demonstrate these qualities?
3. Discuss Ann Judson's prayer: "Direct me in Thy service, and I ask no more. I would not choose my position of

work, or place of labor. Only let me know Thy will, and I will readily comply."

4. Ann Judson provided a voice for those who had no voice. What group of "voiceless women" has God placed on your heart? In what ways are you willing to be their voice?

Chapter Ten

1. Priscilla and her husband responded to ministry opportunities. What opportunities has God placed on your heart? How do you feel led to respond?

2. The words *brave, feisty, opinionated,* and *industrious* describe Katherine von Bora. Martin Luther described her as his "pious and true wife on whom a husband's heart can rely." How can these descriptions depict the same woman?

3. History honors Susanna Wesley for her faith and godly parenting. Read Hebrews 11:4–11, 17–31, and 32–38 and give examples of God's definition of "notoriety" versus the world's definition.

4. Susanna Wesley said: "[We] can have no repose, no peace, no joy, but in loving and being loved by him." How does Susanna's statement relate to our rush to possess and experience more in life?

Chapter Eleven

1. Jerome said Marcella and Paula kept him on his toes with questions about the Bible and challenged him when his answers didn't satisfy. How does a Christian move

from indifference to God's Word to a hunger for God's Word?

2. Read Romans 13:1–7, then discuss ways political service can serve God. Communicate ways to pray for those in governmental leadership.

3. Read John 15:18 and discuss how a Christian can effectively relate to others in today's hedonistic world.

4. Read Matthew 19:16–26. In what areas do you struggle with stewardship? Discuss Jesus's response to the astonished disciples in verse 26.

Chapter Twelve

1. Hilda influenced many lives. Name mentors God has placed in your own life, then share ways you might spiritually invest in the life of another woman.

2. A Christian heritage is a priceless gift from God. What influence has your heritage had on your life? What spiritual blessings do you desire for your children and grandchildren?

3. "God's image carved in ebony" offers a loving tribute to Amanda Smith's life. Read 1 Corinthians 3:10–15 and discuss how to build a life with gold, silver, and costly stones.

4. Read Jeremiah 29:13. How can a believer maintain an ongoing lifestyle of truth-seeking?

Chapter Thirteen

1. Read John 17:1–26 and note the heart of Jesus. What does Christ pray for in John 17:17? The Greek word for

sanctify is *hagiazo*, meaning "to set apart for sacred use" or "to make holy." How does God's Word sanctify?

2. In what ways do you see your life as part of the legacy of faithful women "set apart" to serve God?

3. Many women throughout the world can't read, and many have never heard the name of Jesus. Count the number of Bibles you own and take time to thank God for them.

4. Read 1 John 2:1 and discuss what Jesus communicates to the Father when he intercedes for repentant sinners. Share a time someone interceded for you and how it impacted your life.

Chapter Fourteen

1. Read instructions in 1 Corinthians 11:28–29 for sharing the Lord's Supper in a God-honoring way. How do you "examine yourself" before taking the Lord's Supper?

2. When have you viewed a movie or work of art that caused you to respond with thanksgiving to Christ's death?

3. Name a time when God used someone to communicate truths of Christ's death, burial, and resurrection that brought you to a deeper understanding of salvation.

4. Share memories of when you accepted God's gift of salvation. If you still have questions, review the appendix, "Putting It All Together."

Chapter Fifteen

1. Love for Christ grows in proportion to our knowledge of him. How does a Christian come to know God better?

Why would knowing God parallel growth in love for God?

2. What fears handicap your walk of faith? What does 1 Peter 5:7 say about anxiety? How would you guide another woman in releasing her fears to God?

3. "Moving out of the crowd" requires courage and faith. Name an area where God wants you to move out of the crowd. What keeps you from obedience?

4. Each woman possesses a sphere of influence—the relationships of work, friends, and family. These relationships provide opportunities for publicly living your life of faith. With whom do you hesitate to share God's love? Why?

Chapter Sixteen

1. Read Colossians 3:9–12 and discuss how someone moves from *knowing* their value to Christ to *feeling* valued by God.

2. If you missed out on nurture and affirmation from your father, what voids, if any, do you feel as an adult? Discuss the role of God's Word and the body of Christ in the healing journey.

3. In what ways have you experienced the fellowship and spiritual growth that come from gathering with believers?

4. Bringing your thoughts and yielded heart to an image of the crucifixion scene provides a wonderful way to worship. How has the imagery of worshiping at the foot of the cross affected your personal times with the Lord?

Linda Lesniewski is the women's minister at Green Acres Baptist Church. She is a trainer for LifeWay Resources and a frequent speaker at women's leadership conferences and training seminars. She is a contributing author for *Transformed Lives: Taking Women's Ministry to the Next Level* and the editor of a series of five women's devotional books. She lives in Tyler, Texas.

Also from LINDA LESNIEWSKI

DISCOVER *the* HEART
of WOMEN'S MINISTRY

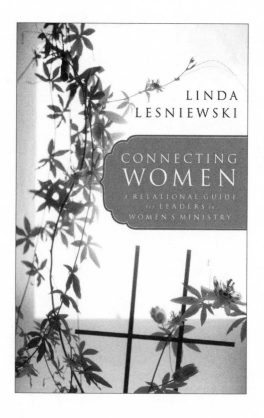

 BakerBooks

a division of Baker Publishing Group
www.bakerbooks.com

AVAILABLE AT YOUR LOCAL BOOKSTORE